AF249033

THE SPIRIT

IN THE EPISTLES

WITNESS LEE

Living Stream Ministry
Anaheim, CA

© 2001 Living Stream Ministry

All rights reserved. No part of this work may be reproduced or transmitted in any form or by any means—graphic, electronic, or mechanical, including photocopying, recording, or information storage and retrieval systems—without written permission from the publisher.

First Edition, February 2001.

ISBN 0-7363-1189-0

Published by

Living Stream Ministry
2431 W. La Palma Ave., Anaheim, CA 92801 U.S.A.
P. O. Box 2121, Anaheim, CA 92814 U.S.A.

Printed in the United States of America

01 02 03 04 05 06 07 / 10 9 8 7 6 5 4 3 2 1

CONTENTS

PREFACE

This book is a translation of messages given in Chinese by Brother Witness Lee, first published in *The Ministry of the Word* in 1966 and 1968. These messages were not reviewed by the speaker.

PART ONE

THE SPIRIT IN THE EPISTLES

CHAPTER ONE

THE LORD BEING THE LIFE-GIVING SPIRIT

And she will bear a son, and you shall call His name Jesus, for it is He who will save His people from their sins. Now all this has happened so that what was spoken by the Lord through the prophet might be fulfilled, saying, "Behold, the virgin shall be with child and shall bear a son, and they shall call His name Emmanuel" (which is translated, God with us). (Matt. 1:21-23)

We all know that here the Lord has two particular names: one is *Jesus,* which means "Savior," and the other is *Emmanuel,* which means "God with us." This One is God with us.

For where there are two or three gathered into My name, there am I in their midst. (18:20)

Go therefore and disciple all the nations, baptizing them into the name of the Father and of the Son and of the Holy Spirit, teaching them to observe all that I have commanded you. And behold, I am with you all the days until the consummation of the age. (28:19-20)

Please take notice that the book of Matthew, the first book of the Gospels, refers three times to the Lord's being with us. The first time is at the beginning, where it says that the Lord's name is called "God with us." The second time is in the middle, where the Lord promised that whenever we are gathered into His name, He would be with us. The last time is at the end, where He promised to be with us until the consummation of the age.

In the beginning was the Word, and the Word was with God, and the Word was God....And the Word became flesh and tabernacled [dwelt] among us...full of grace and reality. (John 1:1, 14)

In the beginning was the Word, and this Word was not only with God but He was God. One day this Word became flesh and dwelt among us, full of grace and reality.

In Him was life, and the life was the light of men. (1:4)

In the Word, the incarnated Word, was life.

I have come that they may have life and may have it abundantly. (10:10)

The purpose of His coming was for man to have life and to have it abundantly.

And I will ask the Father, and He will give you another Comforter, that He may be with you forever, even the Spirit of reality, whom the world cannot receive, because it does not behold Him or know Him; but you know Him, because He abides with you and shall be in you. (14:16-17)

Here we see that the Lord's presence goes a step further. Not only is He with us outwardly, but He will enter into us to abide in us.

I will not leave you as orphans; I am coming to you. Yet a little while and the world beholds Me no longer, but you behold Me; because I live, you also shall live. (vv. 18-19)

In that day you will know that I am in My Father, and you in Me, and I in you. (v. 20)

When therefore it was evening on that day, the first day of the week, and while the doors were shut where the disciples were for fear of the Jews, Jesus came and stood in the midst and said to them, Peace be to you. And when He had said this, He showed them His hands and His side. The disciples therefore rejoiced at seeing the Lord. Then Jesus said to them again, Peace be to you; as the Father has sent Me, I also send you. And when He had said this, He breathed into them and said to them, Receive the Holy Spirit. (20:19-22)

And they passed through the region of Phrygia and Galatia, having been forbidden by the Holy Spirit to speak the word in Asia. And when they had come to Mysia, they tried to go into Bithynia, yet the Spirit of Jesus did not allow them. (Acts 16:6-7)

Notice the two different titles of the Holy Spirit in this passage. Verse 6 speaks of "the Holy Spirit," whereas verse 7 refers to "the Spirit of Jesus." This shows that at this time the

Spirit of Jesus was the Holy Spirit, and the Holy Spirit was the Spirit of Jesus.

> But you are not in the flesh, but in the spirit, if indeed the Spirit of God dwells in you. Yet if anyone does not have the Spirit of Christ, he is not of Him. But if Christ is in you, though the body is dead because of sin, the spirit is life because of righteousness. And if the Spirit of the One who raised Jesus from the dead dwells in you, He who raised Christ Jesus from the dead will also give life to your mortal bodies through His Spirit who indwells you. (Rom. 8:9-11)

It clearly shows here that the Spirit of God is the Spirit of Christ, the Spirit of Christ is Christ Himself, and this Christ is dwelling in us. Brothers and sisters, you need to be very clear about this point. Never think that only the Holy Spirit is dwelling in us. Here it says that Christ is in us because He is the Spirit, who was the Spirit of God but who is now the Spirit of Christ and the Spirit of Jesus.

> The last Adam became a life-giving Spirit. (1 Cor. 15:45)

Life-giving Spirit is a better rendering than *quickening Spirit* (KJV). The last Adam is the Lord Jesus as a man. The Lord Jesus first became a man and then became a life-giving Spirit.

EMMANUEL—GOD WITH MAN

We all know that the first part of the New Testament consists of the Gospels. The subject of the Gospels has two main points, one being the kingdom and the other being life. The kingdom is God's demand, whereas life is God's supply. The demand of the kingdom is much higher than the requirement of the law. The law says, "An eye for an eye, and a tooth for a tooth"; whereas, the kingdom demands that we turn our other cheek to the one who strikes us, yield our cloak to the one who sues us, and go the second mile with the one who compels us. Therefore, no one can meet such demands. Hence, we need the supply of life. Only when God comes into us to be our life can we answer His demands for the kingdom. Only when God supplies Himself as life to us can we meet His demands. Therefore, among the four Gospels, Matthew, a book on the kingdom, is a representative book, and John, a book on life, is also a representative book.

These two representative books, however, have two similar points. First, both mention the Lord's origin. Matthew refers to the Lord's origin and so does John. Of course, we know that Matthew refers to the origin of the Lord as a man, as the seed of David, whereas John refers to the origin of the Lord as God, as the Son of God. The view of Matthew is from the angle of the seed of David, whereas the view of John is from the angle of the Son of God. Both are concerned with the Lord's origin. Although the angles are different, they both tell us that this One is God. From the angle of His being a man, He is God; also from the angle of His being the Son of God, He is God. He was the son of David, yet His name would be called Jesus, that is, Jehovah coming to be our Savior. As the Son of God, He became flesh, yet He is God who was in the beginning.

Second, both books speak about this One coming to be with us. Matthew says that He is Emmanuel, God with us. Wherever we who belong to Him are gathered, there He is with us. Moreover, He is with us until the consummation of the age. John goes further to say that He is with us not only outwardly, to be in our midst, but also inwardly, to be with us forever. Because both of them speak about this presence, neither of them mentions the Lord's ascension. Both Mark and Luke speak about the Lord's ascension because they do not refer to the matter of His presence. Mark tells us at the end that the Lord was taken up into heaven to the right hand of God. Luke also tells us that the Lord was carried up into heaven. Matthew and John, however, specifically deal with the matter of the Lord's presence; therefore, the Lord cannot leave us.

These two books both speak about the Lord's origin at the beginning and refer to the Lord's presence at the end. Brothers and sisters, this is not a small matter. If you want to know the kingdom of God, you must know that there is One who was God and who became flesh to be the seed of David. This One who was God yet man became flesh as the seed of David in order that He might be with us as our Emmanuel. He is with us not only momentarily but even constantly until the consummation of the age, when we will be with Him face to face. Of course, then He will be with us to a fuller degree. Prior to the realization of His outward face-to-face presence, His invisible presence within us will continue until the consummation of this age. John shows us that if we want to enjoy, touch, and experience Him as life, we must see that He is God who came to be with us and who even came into us to be with us. His being with us inwardly is so that we may have life and may have it more abundantly.

AS OUR SAVIOR AND OUR LIFE

I hope that the brothers and sisters can understand this point. The Lord is God who became flesh so that He could be with us, but His ultimate purpose is to come into us to be with us inwardly. His being with us in this way is to be not only our Savior but also our life. If all He wants is only to be our Savior, then He only needs to be in our midst and be with us outwardly. However, since He wants to be our life also, He must come into us to be with us.

Here a question arises: How can He come into us? In His body He could only be among us and could not be within us. He could offer His body as a sacrifice on the cross to accomplish redemption for us and be our Savior, but He could not come into us in His body to be our life. Yet His being our Savior is for Him to be our life, and His being with us outwardly is for Him to come into us to be with us inwardly. Now you can understand that there is a prerequisite here, namely, that He had to die and enter into resurrection. It is through such death and resurrection that He became a Spirit—the life-giving Spirit.

THE GENERAL SUBJECT
OF THE NEW TESTAMENT EPISTLES—
THE LIFE-GIVING SPIRIT

Many Christians have neglected this matter. There is a verse in the Bible that has been ignored by most Christians, and that is 1 Corinthians 15:45b: "The last Adam became a life-giving Spirit." Everyone knows that 1 Corinthians 15 is an important chapter that deals particularly with the matter of resurrection. We all pay attention to the matter of resurrection, but we do not notice what is stated in verse 45. Little do we know that this statement is the subject of all the Epistles of the New Testament. The general subject of more than twenty epistles in the entire New Testament, from the book of Romans and including the seven epistles in the book of Revelation, is the life-giving Spirit.

The four Gospels are on Christ as the Word of God, while the Epistles are on Christ as the life-giving Spirit. In the Gospels the Lord Jesus is the Word; in the Epistles He is the Spirit. The Word is for us to understand, apprehend, know, and grasp. The Spirit is for us to experience, enjoy, and touch. The Word is for revelation, and the Spirit is for life. The first step which the Lord Jesus took in the New Testament was to come as the Word to explain and reveal God, whom we need to understand, apprehend, know, and grasp. Then the next step was that He became the Spirit, whom we need to experience and enjoy as our life. He is the Word for revelation, and He is the Spirit for life. The four Gospels all speak of His being the Word, and all the Epistles speak of His being the Spirit. In this training we want to see the Spirit in the Epistles.

Between the Gospels and the Epistles there is the book of Acts, which is a bridge that takes us from this bank to that bank. The Gospels are on this bank, the Epistles are on that bank, and the Acts is the bridge in the middle. The Lord Jesus was the Word of God, but now He has become the life-giving Spirit. In the Gospels He is the Word, but after crossing the bridge of the Acts, on the bank of the Epistles He is the Spirit.

The Lord said, "The words which I have spoken to you are spirit and are life" (John 6:63b). The words must become the Spirit to be our life. This principle still exists today. When you listen to messages, study the Bible, and read spiritual books, you are receiving the Lord's words. These words, however, must become the Spirit in order to be life to you.

Here we need to realize that in His resurrection He entered into glory. He entered into glory before His ascension; that is, once He was resurrected, He was glorified. Many

Christians think that the Lord Jesus first ascended to heaven and then He was glorified; this is a wrong concept. Rather, He was glorified at the very moment He resurrected. Luke 24:26 says, "Was it not necessary for the Christ to suffer these things and enter into His glory?" Therefore, as soon as He was resurrected, He was glorified. Dear brothers and sisters, notice that He became the life-giving Spirit when He entered into glory. In His incarnation He was a man, the seed of David. However, through His death and resurrection He has become the Spirit. Prior to His resurrection, He was a man in the flesh; after His death and resurrection, He is the Spirit.

THE SPIRIT OF GOD AND THE LIFE-GIVING SPIRIT

There is a big question here. God is Spirit. Then one day this God who is Spirit became flesh to be a man and went through death and resurrection to become a life-giving Spirit. May I ask you, are the Spirit of God and the life-giving Spirit two Spirits? No, they are still one Spirit, but Their elements are different. They are one and the same Spirit, but in one stage the Spirit is the Spirit of God and in another stage He is the life-giving Spirit, the Spirit of Jesus, the Spirit of Christ. For example, if I put a white handkerchief into a blue dye and then take it out after five minutes, it is still the same handkerchief, but now it has become a blue handkerchief. The white handkerchief and the blue handkerchief are not two handkerchiefs; they are one handkerchief in two stages. In the first stage it is a white handkerchief, and in the latter stage it is a blue handkerchief. In the first stage there are fewer elements; in the latter stage there are more elements. In the same manner, the Spirit of God and the Spirit of Jesus are one Spirit in two stages. Originally He was the Spirit of God, but after the Lord's incarnation, death, and resurrection, the Spirit of God became the life-giving Spirit.

The second question is this: In the first stage, was there life in the Spirit of God? Yes, there was. But in the first stage could the Spirit of God give life? No, He could not. Therefore, in the first stage the Spirit of God was the Spirit of life, but He could not give life. Why? It is because the Lord had not passed through death and resurrection. Here we need a further explanation. Death and resurrection involve two matters. First, death and resurrection solved all the problems between us and God, such as our sins, the flesh, the world, and Satan, who is always hindering and troubling us from behind the scene. God wants to give us life, yet we are evil and corrupt, and there are also the world and Satan's hindrance. Therefore, God must first remove these things. The Lord's death solved these problems for us. Besides this, we also know that any life that is to be given to men must first be released. Therefore, John 12:24 says, "Unless the grain of wheat falls into the ground and dies, it abides alone; but if it dies, it bears much fruit." The grain of wheat has life, but unless it goes through death and grows forth again, it cannot impart its life into many grains.

Therefore, dear brothers and sisters, before His incarnation, death, and resurrection, the Lord was life and in Him was life, yet He could not give life. But when He removed all the problems between us and God and released the life in Him through death and resurrection, then He became a life-giving Spirit.

Now we are no longer in the Gospels but have come to the Epistles. We have covered the Old Testament and the Gospels, and we have also crossed the bridge—the Acts. I am not speaking these things in a careless way. When studying the Bible, we need to follow its line. Acts chapters one and two speak of the Holy Spirit, and chapter sixteen still refers to the Holy Spirit (v. 6), but immediately after referring to the Holy Spirit, it shifts to the Spirit of Jesus (v. 7). In Acts 16 the title *the Spirit of Jesus* appears. Who is the Spirit of Jesus? The Spirit of Jesus is the Holy Spirit and the Spirit of God. But strictly speaking, the Spirit of God was there before the death and resurrection of the Son of God, whereas the Spirit of Jesus came into being after the Son had become flesh, passed through death to deal with man's sins, and was resurrected to release His life. This is just like the illustration given above. The blue handkerchief is the white handkerchief in the beginning; at that time the white handkerchief did not have the element of blue color, but now it does. The Spirit of Jesus is the Spirit of God, but praise the Lord, today we are not in the Old Testament, nor in the Gospels, nor in the Acts. Instead, we are in the Epistles, which speak about the Triune God, who became flesh and passed through death and resurrection in the Son through the Spirit, being a life-giving Spirit today.

LAYING STRESS ON THE LIFE-GIVING SPIRIT

I believe the brothers and sisters understand that this is very different from the concept of most believers. Now you know that the Spirit in the New Testament Epistles is the Spirit of God and the Spirit of Jesus Christ. I hope you will remember that the Spirit of Jesus is in Acts 16:7, the Spirit of Christ is in Romans 8:9, and the Spirit of Jesus Christ is in Philippians 1:19. Today the Spirit of God is not merely the Spirit of God but also the Spirit of Jesus, the Spirit of Christ, and the Spirit of Jesus Christ. More than twenty of the epistles, including the epistles in Revelation, all speak about this Spirit. The problems in the church today are due to the fact that we do not have adequate knowledge of this Spirit, and the weakness in the church is also due to this inadequacy.

Ever since the time of Martin Luther, God has recovered many items in the church, but the recovery concerning the knowledge and experience of this Spirit are still insufficient. When the Brethren were raised up by God in 1828, they mostly emphasized the recovery of God's Word. They indeed had a considerable amount of the recovery of God's Word, but they greatly neglected the Spirit. Hence, their spiritual condition was dead. The Bible says that the letter deadens and kills. This word is indeed true.

Recently while visiting several local churches, we noticed that a certain locality was putting much emphasis on studying the Bible. There are several Bible-study meetings during the week, but there is not one prayer meeting. Please do not blame me for daring to say conclusively that if a church only studies the Bible, reads the Scriptures, and reads spiritual books, then the more it reads and studies, the more it will become dead. There is no exception to this. I cannot say that this is evident in the history of two thousand years, but I can say that it is clearly proven in the history of the five hundred years since the time of Luther's Reformation. Any church that overemphasizes the reading of the Word, the studying of the Bible, and the researching of spiritual truths always ends in death.

Oh, brothers and sisters, the Lord's words must be the Spirit to be life! How can the words become the Spirit? The only way is by prayer. You must turn into prayer the words which you have read. You must pray. We would rather have two prayer meetings and one Bible-study meeting weekly. Our lack today is not in words but in the Spirit. We are not weak in words. Rather, we are too weak in our spirit; our spirit is not released. It is true that the truths can make you steady. Without the Spirit, however, this steadiness will become dullness, and dullness eventually becomes death. Therefore, we must have the Spirit. Brothers, I repeat, any place that pays attention only to truths, doctrines, and knowledge will end up in death. There are too many examples of this, and there is no exception to this. Many are in their mind caring for knowledge without any stirring in their spirit. Brothers and sisters, where are we today? Are we in the Old Testament, in the Gospels, or on the bridge of the Acts? Or have we crossed the bridge and arrived at the Epistles? What good is it to merely emphasize the accuracy and profoundness of doctrines? Vitality is in the Spirit, not in doctrines.

Thank the Lord that He recovered many doctrines through the Brethren. Eventually, however, the Brethren became dead due to their leaning heavily on doctrines. At that very time, which was around the middle of the nineteenth century, a reaction arose, which was the Pentecostal movement. The Pentecostal people are indeed living, but they are on the wrong way. Instead of touching the Spirit in the Epistles, they touch the Spirit in Acts, and not only so, the way they take is not proper. I do not dare to say that their activities are one hundred percent false, but I dare say that over ninety percent of them are false. Only one out of one hundred cases of tongue-speakings is true. Nevertheless, in Christianity, because the Brethren were dead in their doctrines and the denominations were empty in their rituals, the Pentecostal movement conveniently came in to fill the void.

Dear brothers and sisters, nothing can stop the Pentecostal movement as a counterfeit except the life-giving Spirit. In the Bible, Romans is a book on the Christian life, living, and service. In this book, which is an outline of the truth, is speaking in tongues mentioned anywhere? Ephesians is a book exclusively on the church, but is speaking in tongues mentioned anywhere? Speaking in tongues is not mentioned at all in Galatians, Philippians, Colossians, 1 and 2 Thessalonians, 1 and 2 Timothy, Titus, Hebrews, 1 and 2 Peter, and even to the end of Revelation. Then you may ask, "Is speaking in tongues not mentioned in 1 Corinthians?" Yes, but it is mentioned in a way of pouring cold water on it and not in a way of encouragement. What did Paul say? He seemed to be saying, "You do not lack in any gift. You have speaking in tongues, interpreting of tongues, and healing, yet you are fleshly and you are infants in Christ. When I came to you, I did not determine to know anything among you except Jesus Christ, and this One crucified. When did I direct your attention to the gifts? I have directed your attention only to the Lord Jesus and this One crucified. Only Christ is God's wisdom and God's power." Paul did not say that the outward gifts were wrong. Rather, he wanted the Corinthian believers to turn from the outward gifts to the inner life. Therefore, following this, 2 Corinthians shows us that the apostle Paul had a thorn in the flesh for which he entreated the Lord three times that it might depart from him. Nevertheless, the Lord seemed to say, "No, I will not remove the thorn because I want you to experience Me as the sufficient grace. In the early days when you preached the gospel, I used you to heal diseases and cast out demons to prove that I am the mighty and true Lord. Even your handkerchief could heal diseases. Nevertheless, I will not remove the thorn that has come to you. I want you to turn from the outward gifts to the inward life." This is why 2 Corinthians speaks a great deal about sufferings, afflictions, the outer man's being consumed, and the inner man's being renewed day by day.

Dear brothers and sisters, in the Epistles God wants us to leave the outward gifts and turn to the inner life, which is the life-giving Spirit. Every one of us must see this. Because the church fell into a situation of empty rituals and empty doctrines of letters, the Pentecostal movement appeared. Pentecostalism conveniently fills the void left by rituals and doctrines, both of which are empty. But history tells us that in the last one hundred years the Pentecostal movement did not accomplish anything. Those of us who are from the northern part of China know that the Pentecostal movement was very prevailing for a period of time there, but it did not accomplish anything. On the contrary, what it left behind was a mess, and everything was in confusion. It did not leave a proper way for people to take or a proper testimony for people to see. Anything that is genuine will last, while anything that is false will be short-lived. This is true not only of China, but it is also true of England. Where are the Pentecostal churches in England today? You cannot find any. If you go to America, the Pentecostal movement there is also a mess. There are false things, fabricated things, and confusion.

Brothers and sisters, do not think that I am here attacking anything. May the Lord be merciful to us. I simply have a burden within me to show the children of God the right path. The right path lies with the life-giving Spirit. Even if the outward outpouring of the Holy Spirit is genuine, it is at most merely to meet a one-time need, but I am not convinced that there is such a need in today's church. I repeat, the subject of the Epistles from the first one to the last is the life-giving Spirit. Therefore, our present need is to know and experience Him. In the past ages God has recovered considerably His Word and the outward Spirit. I believe that today He is recovering in great measure the inward Spirit.

Chapter Two

ROMANS

> For if we, being enemies, were reconciled to God through the death of His Son, much more we will be saved in His life, having been reconciled. (Rom. 5:10)

In this verse of the Scriptures two matters are mentioned: the first matter is the death of God's Son, and the second is His life. This verse tells us that while we were enemies of God, we were reconciled to God through the death of the Lord Jesus and the problems between us and God were solved. Moreover, since we have been reconciled, we will be saved in the life of the Lord Jesus. Being reconciled to God through the Lord's death is one thing and being saved in the Lord's life is another thing. Here, our being saved refers not only to our being saved by believing in the Lord, but even more to our being saved by the Lord step by step, after we believe in Him, from the old creation and the self into His glory. On the negative side, we were saved through the Lord's death to be reconciled to God, thereby solving the problems between us and God. On the positive side, we are being saved in the Lord's life from the old creation and the natural being to enter fully into the glory of God.

> And not only so, but also boasting in God through our Lord Jesus Christ, through whom we have now received the reconciliation. (v. 11)

In this verse *whom* refers to the One who is in resurrection. The Greek word for *boasting* means "to boast" and also "to exult." This is to say that since we were reconciled to God through the Lord's death, we now have God as our boast, our exultation, our rejoicing, and our enjoyment in the Lord's resurrection through His life.

For the law of the Spirit of life has freed me in Christ Jesus from the law of sin and of death. (8:2)

That the righteous requirement of the law might be fulfilled in us, who do not walk according to the flesh but according to the spirit. For those who are according to the flesh mind the things of the flesh; but those who are according to the spirit, the things of the Spirit. For the mind set on the flesh is death, but the mind set on the spirit is life and peace. (vv. 4-6)

But you are not in the flesh, but in the spirit, if indeed the Spirit of God dwells in you. Yet if anyone does not have the Spirit of Christ, he is not of Him. But if Christ is in you, though the body is dead because of sin, the spirit is life because of righteousness. And if the Spirit of the One who raised Jesus from the dead dwells in you, He who raised Christ Jesus from the dead will also give life to your mortal bodies through His Spirit who indwells you. (vv. 9-11)

For you have not received a spirit of slavery bringing you into fear again, but you have received a spirit of sonship in which we cry, Abba, Father! The Spirit Himself witnesses with our spirit that we are children of God. (vv. 15-16)

And not only so, but we ourselves also, who have the first-fruits of the Spirit, even we ourselves groan in ourselves, eagerly awaiting sonship, the redemption of our body. (v. 23)

Moreover, in like manner the Spirit also joins in to help us in our weakness, for we do not know for what we should pray as is fitting, but the Spirit Himself intercedes for us with groanings which cannot be uttered. But He who searches the hearts knows what the mind of the Spirit is, because He intercedes for the saints according to God. And we know that all things work together for good to those who love God, to those who are called according to His purpose. Because those whom He foreknew, He also predestinated to be conformed to the image of His Son, that He might be the Firstborn among many brothers; and those whom He predestinated, these He also called; and those whom He called, these He also justified; and those whom He justified, these He also glorified. (vv. 26-30)

Concerning His Son, who came out of the seed of David according to the flesh, who was designated the Son of God in power according to the Spirit of holiness out of the resurrection of the dead, Jesus Christ our Lord. (1:3-4)

I exhort you therefore, brothers, through the compassions of God to present your bodies a living sacrifice, holy, well-pleasing to God, which is your reasonable service. (12:1)

For the kingdom of God is not eating and drinking, but righteousness and peace and joy in the Holy Spirit. (14:17)

Holy here is an emphasized word. In Greek *Holy* comes after *the Spirit,* meaning that the Spirit is the "Holy"; hence, the Holy Spirit.

THE KEY TO THE BOOK OF ROMANS

Romans is a book that particularly gives an outline of the Christian life. It speaks clearly concerning three great matters to which every Christian must pay attention. The first great matter concerns our salvation or, we may say, justification. The second great matter is on how we should live in the Spirit after we have been saved. The third matter is on how, by such a living, we may become living members to live the church life, the Body life. It speaks first about our salvation, then about our living in the Spirit, and then about our service and coordination in the Body. Our salvation is for us to live in the Spirit, and by living in the Spirit we become living members coordinating in the Body. Therefore, living in the Spirit is the key to the Body life.

Formerly we were sinners and also enemies of God. We offended Him and had a problem with Him. The Lord Jesus, however, reconciled us to God by dying for us sinners and solving the problems between us and God. Therefore, today when we believe in the Lord, we are justified and have no more problems with God. This is what the Lord's death has accomplished for us. After we have been saved, we have the life of the Lord Jesus in us. First, this life sets us free from all kinds of bondage, such as the world, the flesh, the law of sin, and the old creation. Second, this life is saving us. With regard to our bondage, we need to be freed; with regard to our fallen condition, we need to be saved. The Lord Jesus is doing the work not only of setting us free to deliver us from all kinds of bondage but also of saving us day by day and moment by moment so that we may come out of our fallen situation. Third, He is doing the work of transformation. Fourth,

He is doing the work of sanctification to set us apart and make us holy so that we may be separated from all things and all worldly people. Fifth, eventually He will glorify us to make us as glorious as He is. Dear brothers and sisters, all these items are included in our being saved in the life of the Lord Jesus. Our salvation through the death of the Lord Jesus resolves the problems we had with God in the past. Our being saved in the life of the Lord allows Him to work in us to set us free, to save us, to transform us, to sanctify us, and to glorify us. How does the Lord Jesus carry out all these works in us? It all hinges on His being a living Spirit. Hence, the first section of Romans shows us that the Lord Jesus died for us on the cross, and the second section shows us that He is in us living instead of us. Previously Christ died on the cross, but now He is living in us.

The clause in the beginning of Romans 8:10, "Christ is in you," is a great word; it is the key to the entire book of Romans. God works to such an extent that Christ is wrought into us, and this Christ who is in us is the Spirit. In Romans this Spirit has four different titles: first, the Spirit of life; second, the Spirit of sonship; third, the Spirit of firstfruits; and fourth, the Spirit of holiness. If you have a clear view of these few points, then you have grasped the key to Romans. Over the years, among the children of God many books were written concerning Romans, but the key to this book was never clearly pointed out. At this time I hope to impress you with this crucial point. The key to this book is "Christ in you," and this Christ is the Spirit.

Some may ask, "How can Christ be this Spirit?" This is a mystery that is hard to explain thoroughly. Second Corinthians 3:17 says that "the Lord is the Spirit"; then it goes on to refer to "the Spirit of the Lord." On the one hand, it says that "the Lord is the Spirit"; hence, the Lord and the Spirit are one. On the other hand, it mentions "the Spirit of the Lord"; hence, the Lord and the Spirit are two. However, the two aspects are mentioned together. Furthermore, John 1:1 says, "In the beginning was the Word, and the Word was with God, and the Word was God." When it says that the Word was with God, it means that the Word and God are two. Yet it also says that the Word was God, meaning that They are one. Therefore, They are two yet one and one yet two. Although we do not understand this doctrine, we still need to accept this fact. The Christ who dwells in us is the Spirit.

THE SPIRIT OF LIFE

The Lord said, "I have come that they may have life and may have it abundantly" (John 10:10). How does the Lord give us this life? It is by His being in us as the Spirit of life. Basically, the work of the Lord as the Spirit in us is to be the Spirit of life. Receiving this life is not a once-for-all matter. Just as an infant after his birth still needs a daily supply for his life to be sustained and to grow, so we who have received the Lord as our life also need to receive His supply daily. The Lord is supplying us within daily by being the Spirit of life in us.

The most important thing which the Lord as the Spirit of life is doing in us is to release us from the law of sin and of death. When you are in your spirit and not in your knowledge or thoughts, when you are in your spirit and not in your emotions or preferences, when you are in your spirit and not in your opinions, when you live in your spirit and turn to your spirit to contact the Spirit of life, the result is that you are released.

Previously we gave many messages on dealing with sins. Today I would like to tell you that there is a simple secret here. Do you want to overcome your weaknesses? Do you want to overcome your entangling temper? The simple secret is to turn yourself back to your spirit. Forget your weaknesses, failures, and shortcomings. Do not pay attention to them. Instead, turn yourself back to your spirit. Whenever you turn to the spirit and touch the spirit, you have the supply of the Spirit of life. As a result, spontaneously you are set free. We often say that we need to deal with the self. It is not wrong to say this. However, if we pay too much attention to the self, then if we are not careful, we may instead be entangled by the self. Sometimes the more we deal with the self, the more we are in the self. Therefore, instead of paying too much attention to your self, you need to turn to your spirit. The Lord, who is the life-giving Spirit, becomes your supply when you turn to your spirit to contact Him. The result is that you are set free from your self.

Most of us have made this mistake in principle: We like to deal with the problems and neglect the contact with our spirit and the moving in our spirit. In the book of Romans, Paul did not deal with those matters. Instead, he told us to walk according to the spirit. When we walk according to the spirit by turning to the spirit, all the problems will be solved neatly and all the difficulties will be dealt with spontaneously.

Romans 8:6 says, "For the mind set on the flesh is death, but the mind set on the spirit is life and peace." This means that if you set your mind on the flesh, the result will be death, but if you set your mind on the spirit, the result will be life and peace. In other words, if your mind pays attention to the flesh, that will be death, and if your mind pays attention to the spirit, that will be life and peace.

You may consider this picture: We human beings are of three parts—the spirit being the innermost part, the soul being in the middle, and the body being the outermost part. Due to the addition of sin, the body has become the flesh. Although the mind is a part of the soul, it represents man's personality. When a person is saved, his spirit is regenerated by the entrance of the Spirit of life. The mind represents man himself. When the mind stands with the flesh, this means that the mind is set on the flesh and the result is death. When the mind stands with the spirit, this means that the mind is set on the spirit and the result is life and peace. Regardless of whether the flesh is good or bad, if you pay attention to it, the result will be death. If your mind gives heed to the spirit, the result will be life.

According to this basic principle, many teachings in Christianity are good, but they lead people to pay attention to things outside of the spirit. Hence, the result is failure. The way of victory, the way of life, is to reject anything outside of the Lord. Do you have a temper? Do not pay attention to your temper; rather, turn your mind back to focus on the spirit and to be set on the spirit. There you have the life-giving Spirit. In the past we did not know this secret adequately. This is why many spiritual teachings were still turning people's attention to the things outside of the spirit. At this time we must see that we need to turn our mind back to focus on the spirit and to be set on the spirit. Here you will touch the source of life, which is the life-giving Spirit. Consequently, you have life and peace. When you turn from your spirit to other places and are therefore cut off from the source of the Spirit of life within you, then regardless of how much you have done, everything is death.

Therefore, you must turn to the spirit within and not pay attention to yourself, your failures, your temper, or your flesh. Romans 8 shows us that the Spirit of life in us is Christ. We need to call our mind back to our spirit and constantly pay attention to our spirit. In this way we are living in the spirit and walking according to the spirit. Then the Spirit of life will begin to operate in us to supply, release, and rescue us. Thus, we will be able to overcome.

THE SPIRIT OF SONSHIP

Furthermore, the Spirit of life is also the Spirit of sonship for us to enter into sonship. First, the Spirit of sonship witnesses in you that you are a son of God. Formerly, as a descendant of Adam, you were a sinner, but now since you have the Lord Jesus in you, you have the life of the Son and also the Spirit of the Son. This Spirit of sonship in you proves that you are a son of God. Therefore, after being saved, you can call God your Father. Sometimes when you fall, when you are weak, and when you are far away from God, you think that perhaps God does not care about you anymore. Nevertheless, the Spirit of the divine sonship still witnesses in you that God is your Father and that you belong to God.

Not only so, the Spirit of sonship also leads you within. As many as are led by the Spirit of God, these are sons of God. Regardless of how weak you are as a Christian, often you still have the feeling that perhaps you should not do a certain thing. Sometimes you are not able to overcome and therefore go ahead and do it, yet you know within that you should not have done it because it is not fitting for God's children.

Brothers and sisters, this is the leading of the Spirit of the divine sonship in you.

The Spirit of sonship also sympathizes with us in our weakness. You do not know how to pray, but He prays in you on your behalf with groanings which cannot be uttered. The more you pray, the more He causes you to be like the Son of God, to be conformed to the image of God's Son. Sometimes He also arranges the outward circumstances to match the prayer within so that He may deal with you until you are like the Son of God and have the image of the Lord Jesus. In this way we have the life, the nature, and the Spirit of the Son of God inwardly, and we also have the image of the Son of God outwardly to become God's many sons. The Lord Jesus then becomes the Firstborn among many sons.

Here we can see that sonship is the reality of a son. The Spirit of sonship leads us into the reality of the Son. Today many Christians think that the Lord's salvation will eventually save us into heaven. This concept is inaccurate. Is the concept of going to heaven found in the gospel preached in the book of Romans? No, the book of Romans never tells us to pay attention to a certain place; it never tells us we will go to heaven. This thought is not found in the gospel. The thought in the gospel is that the salvation of the Son of God, together with the Son Himself as the Spirit of life, will make sinners sons of God. Romans 8:29-30 says, "Because those whom He foreknew, He also predestinated to be conformed to the image of His Son, that He might be the Firstborn among many brothers; and those whom He predestinated, these He also called; and those whom He called, these He also justified; and those whom He justified, these He also glorified." Here we see that God's predestination, God's calling, and God's justification are for us to be conformed to the image of His Son that His Son might be the Firstborn among many brothers. As long as God can accomplish this, it does not matter whether He puts His Firstborn and the many sons on earth, in heaven, or in midair; wherever He puts them is good. The purpose of God is not to put us in a certain place but to save us, who are sinners and the sons of disobedience, to such an extent that we become the sons of God. We are not adopted sons; we are His real sons, who are born of Him and are growing by Him to be conformed to His image. This is the divine sonship.

A brother once argued with me about the truth, saying, "Brother Lee, you say that a Christian must overcome so that he will be able to reign with the Lord Jesus in the future. This teaching is wrong. The Bible tells us that every saved one will reign with the Lord." I said, "Brother, let us not talk merely about theories; let us talk about the reality. If the Lord put you on the throne today, do you think you are fit to be a king? Do you look like a king? It is useless to just talk about the doctrine. You have to ask whether you look like a king." I heard that in some European countries with a constitutional monarchy, such as Denmark and Great Britain, a royal prince has to be trained daily from his youth. He has to receive strict training in walking, speaking, and managing affairs. Then one day when he is put on the throne, he will look like a king. Brothers and sisters, it is true that by His mercy and grace we all are sons of God, but if we look at ourselves today, do we look like sons of God? Oh, we are sons of God, but we do not have the sonship! We have the position of a son and are sons of God, but today we do not look like sons. Nevertheless, thank and praise God, the Lord Jesus as the living Spirit in us is making us fit to be sons of God. As the Spirit of sonship, He is leading us to always cry, "Abba, Father!" If in the morning you pray to the Lord Jesus and cry, "Abba, Father," the whole day you will become more like a son of God. A sister may truly love the Lord, but she often may have such a "long face" that it is too much for others to take. She may have a long face not mainly before others but toward her husband. However, I am sure that if this sister would spend ten minutes every morning to call, "Abba, Father," she will no longer make a long face. This is the result of the operation of the Spirit of sonship in her.

Brothers, I do not know what to say to thoroughly express my inner feeling. I repeat, the salvation of God is not merely to save us to be good men but to make us His sons. Hence, God has put His Son in us as the Spirit of sonship to transform us and work in us step by step until we are conformed to the image of His Son. We are not just sons in name but sons in reality. We have not only the Son's life but also the Son's image.

We may all look like people who are very good, but to this day we still do not sufficiently look like the sons of God. Hence, the Spirit of sonship is working in us to minister to us the life of the Son of God. The more the life of the Son of God is ministered into us, the more we are being transformed and conformed into sons of God. Therefore, it is not a matter of improving our outward behavior. Rather, it is a matter of transforming our inward nature. You need to call your mind, your self, back to pay attention to the Spirit. Do not leave the Spirit and pay attention to being victorious, holy, or spiritual. The more you pay attention to being spiritual, the less spiritual you will be. Neither should you focus on your temper, because the more you focus on your temper, the worse your temper will be. You must heed the Spirit; then you will be enlivened within, and He will supply you within that you may have the reality of the Son of God.

THE SPIRIT OF FIRSTFRUITS

No matter how much we enjoy the Spirit of life, what we have enjoyed is only the firstfruits as a foretaste. The great harvest will have to wait until after the Lord's return. The Holy Spirit in us today is the firstfruits, the foretaste. Ephesians chapter one says the Holy Spirit in us is a pledge. The Greek word for *pledge* denotes a token, a sample, a foretaste, or a pledge. Today, regardless of how much you have experienced and enjoyed the Spirit of life, it is just a foretaste. When the Lord comes back, we will enjoy the Spirit of life richly and fully.

Although the enjoyment of the foretaste and the enjoyment of the full taste differ in measure, they are the same in nature. In the coming age what we will enjoy will still be the Spirit of life. The more we enjoy this Spirit by turning to our spirit, the more we taste His supplying, watering, releasing, rescuing, uplifting, and transcending. We can enjoy all these things today.

THE SPIRIT OF HOLINESS

This work of the Holy Spirit is a sanctifying work, a work that makes us holy. What does it mean to be sanctified, to be made holy? Originally we did not have any holiness in us. The good things we had were things of man, and the bad things were sins. However, the Spirit of the divine sonship, who is "the Holy," has come into us and has sanctified us. In Greek, in many passages where the Holy Spirit is mentioned, it is written as "the Spirit, the Holy," meaning that the Spirit is holiness. In the entire universe everything is common; only God Himself is holy. God, who is the Spirit, the Holy, has been mingled with us. Hence, we have been made holy. This is just like adding orange juice, which is yellow, to water, causing the colorless water to be "orange-ized." Oh, dear brothers and sisters, from the day we were saved, this Spirit has come into us to be mingled with us. The more He is mingled with us, the more we are being transformed. The more He is mingled with us, the more we are being sanctified. And the more sanctified we are, the more we are like Him and are conformed to His image.

At the outset, the book of Romans says in chapter one that the gospel which we preach is concerning the Son of God, Jesus Christ our Lord, who came out of the seed of David according to the flesh as a man and who was designated the Son of God in power according to the Spirit of holiness out of the resurrection of the dead. We cannot find this kind of utterance in any of the Epistles other than the book of Romans. Why? The reason is that Romans shows us that the salvation of God makes us, those who are fleshly and wicked, His divine sons. There is a sample, a model, of this, and it is Jesus Christ. When He was in the flesh on the earth, people could not tell that He was the Son of God. But one day, after His death and resurrection, He was completely sanctified by the Spirit of holiness that was within Him. In other words, His whole being was transformed. When He was in the flesh, people recognized Him as Jesus of Nazareth, whose visage and form were marred, who had no attractive form, and who had altogether the appearance of a man. However, after His death and resurrection, He was transformed, sanctified, and designated to be the Son of God by the Spirit of holiness. This is a sample, a pattern, a model. Likewise, we are now in the flesh, and we will also pass through death and resurrection so that we may be transformed and sanctified gradually by the Spirit of holiness to become the many sons of God.

Therefore, please remember that, in the book of Romans, chapter one mentions the Son of God and chapter eight mentions the sons of God. In other words, we have the Son of God in Romans 1 and the sons of God in Romans 8. Previously, the Spirit of holiness sanctified only one person, Jesus the Nazarene, through death and resurrection, sanctifying Him in His flesh to be the Son of God. Now the Spirit of holiness is doing the work of transformation in us also to sanctify us so that we, who were sons of wickedness, may become glorious sons of God. Thus, we are the many sons of God, and the only begotten Son of God becomes the Firstborn among us.

Dear brothers and sisters, we need to come back to the spirit within us every day and every moment, paying attention to nothing but this one thing—following the Spirit. "As many as are led by the Spirit of God, these are sons of God" (Rom. 8:14). We do not deal with this matter or that matter; we only deal with one thing: turning to the spirit, calling our mind back to the spirit, living in the spirit, and walking in the spirit. This is our living.

BURNING AND REJOICING IN SPIRIT

Then, what about our service? We need to be burning and fervent in spirit. It is hard to say whether the word *spirit* in Romans 12:11 denotes the Spirit of God or our spirit. It is the same as the word used for *spirit* in Romans 8:5, 6, and 10. We can serve only when we are fervent and burning in spirit.

Finally, chapter fourteen says that the kingdom of God is not eating and drinking, but righteousness and peace and joy in the Holy Spirit (v. 17). It is right if you can rejoice in the spirit; it is wrong if you cannot rejoice in the spirit. In this uplifted, rejoicing spirit you have the overcoming life, the sanctified life, the spiritual life, the Body life, and the church life.

CONCLUSION

I always have the feeling that in all these years God has done a great deal of recovery in the church. The only item that has not been sufficiently recovered is the Spirit. I believe that from now on our messages and our ministry of the Word will concentrate on this matter. We will speak from the Epistles concerning the Spirit. Justification is for Christ to come into us. Christ's coming into us means that the Spirit of Christ is in us, and this Spirit is the Spirit of life to supply, release, and rescue us. What the Spirit of life is doing is to work the divine sonship, the reality of the Son of God, into us for our transformation so that we may be conformed to the image of God's Son. This is also His sanctifying work to make us, who were sons of wickedness, holy sons of God. This work is the will of God. Today we need to cooperate with this work to become living members, who walk according to the spirit, turn our mind to focus on the spirit, and live in the spirit. We need to be burning in spirit to serve God, and we always need to be rejoicing in spirit. This is the Christians' life and living. This is also the central thought of the book of Romans.

In summary, Romans shows us that the redeeming Christ, the Christ who died on our behalf, is in us today as the life-giving Spirit. He supplies, releases, and rescues us moment by moment, carrying out the work of sonship to transform us into sons of God and conform us to the image of God's Son by sanctifying us. He makes us, who were sons of wickedness, genuine sons of God, sons in name and in reality with His life and His image. Thus, as the many sons of God we become the living members coordinating together to become one Body for the expression of the God of glory. Therefore, today we should take heed to the Spirit by setting our mind on the spirit, paying attention to the spirit, being considerate of the spirit, fervently serving God in the spirit, and always rejoicing in the spirit.

CHAPTER THREE

FIRST CORINTHIANS

CHRIST BEING OUR PORTION

To the church of God which is in Corinth, to those who have been sanctified in Christ Jesus, the called saints, with all those who call upon the name of our Lord Jesus Christ in every place, who is theirs and ours. (1 Cor. 1:2)

Christ "is theirs and ours"—this is a word of great emphasis. Christ is the blessed portion given to us by God, just as the land of Canaan was the blessed portion given to the children of Israel by God. This is our portion, our inheritance.

God is faithful, through whom you were called into the fellowship of His Son, Jesus Christ our Lord. (v. 9)

For indeed Jews require signs and Greeks seek wisdom, but we preach Christ crucified. (vv. 22-23)

Here we see that signs and wisdom may become replacements of Christ. We may want signs or wisdom instead of Christ. Jews require signs and Greeks seek wisdom, but we preach Christ crucified.

But of Him you are in Christ Jesus, who became wisdom to us from God: both righteousness and sanctification and redemption. (v. 30)

After reading these verses, we realize that chapter one shows us how Christ is our portion. Today God has given us Christ to be our everything. What God gives to us is not signs, nor wisdom, nor any other thing, but Christ.

That in everything you were enriched in Him, in all utterance and all knowledge. (v. 5)

So that you do not lack in any gift. (v. 7)

The church in Corinth was enriched in all utterance

and all knowledge and did not lack in any gift, yet the Corinthians were very poor in their spiritual life. This shows that utterance, knowledge, or any gift is not Christ. Utterance, knowledge, signs, and wisdom—all these are not Christ. What God wants to give us is not these things, but Christ. First Corinthians chapter one is a strong chapter in the Bible which proves that Christ is not utterance, knowledge, gifts, signs, or wisdom. This is very clear. You may have all spiritual utterance and all knowledge, you may have various gifts, and you may have signs and wisdom, but you may have missed Christ. You may use these things to replace Christ.

THE HOLY SPIRIT MAKING CHRIST OUR EXPERIENCE

But as it is written, "Things which eye has not seen and ear has not heard and which have not come up in man's heart; things which God has prepared for those who love Him." (1 Cor. 2:9)

What are the things which God has prepared for those who love Him? In my youth I heard people say that these things are related to the blessing of going to heaven. But if you read the New Testament and the context of this passage in 1 Corinthians, you will see that these things denote Christ Himself. The blessing which God has prepared for us is the Spirit of sonship, the life-giving Spirit, who is leading and working in us continually until we are brought into glory. Not to mention that our eyes have not seen and our ears have not heard of this blessing, but even our hearts have never thought about it.

But to us God has revealed them through the Spirit, for the Spirit searches all things, even the depths of God. For who among men knows the things of man, except the spirit of man which is in him? In the same way, the things of God also no one has known except the Spirit of God. (vv. 10-11)

Brothers and sisters, what are the things of God? The things of God are the things concerning Christ, whom God has wrought into our being as the Spirit of sonship to work in us and bring us into glory.

But we have received not the spirit of the world but the Spirit which is from God, that we may know the things which have been graciously given to us by God; which things also we speak, not in words taught by human wisdom but in words taught by the Spirit, interpreting spiritual things with spiritual words. (vv. 12-13)

Here Paul does not speak about dreams or visions but concerning how God accomplished redemption and works His Son into us as the Spirit of sonship to transform, sanctify, and glorify us that we may be like His Son.

> But a soulish man does not receive the things of the Spirit of God, for they are foolishness to him and he is not able to know them because they are discerned spiritually. But the spiritual man discerns all things, but he himself is discerned by no one. For who has known the mind of the Lord and will instruct Him? But we have the mind of Christ." (vv. 14-16)

We see two kinds of men here: One is a spiritual man and the other is a soulish man. A spiritual man is not only regenerated in his spirit, but he also has the mind of Christ in his mind, which is referred to in Romans 12:2 as being transformed by the renewing of the mind.

First Corinthians chapter one is on Christ, and chapter two is on the Spirit. Christ is our portion and our all. Utterance, knowledge, gifts, signs, or wisdom is not Christ. Only Christ Himself is Christ. In a sense, the Jews knew God, but their knowledge was insufficient; they still required signs. The Greeks were active in their mind, and they sought education and wisdom. But the apostles were commissioned by God to preach Christ crucified, not signs required by the Jews or wisdom sought by the Greeks. Only Christ is real wisdom and real power. Just as God had put the children of Israel in the land of Canaan, so God has also put us in Christ and has made Him our wisdom, redemption, righteousness, and sanctification. In other words, God has put us in Christ so that Christ may become our all. Christ is theirs and ours (1 Cor. 1:2). He belongs to all of us who have believed in Him. God has called us into the fellowship of Christ as our portion. All these things are covered in chapter one.

However, I would like to tell you, brothers and sisters, that although the things covered in 1 Corinthians chapter one are perfect, they are merely objective facts and not our subjective experience. Hence, there is the need for chapter two, which is on the Spirit. Chapter two speaks not only about the Spirit of God objectively but also about our spirit subjectively. At the end it concludes by asking whether we are soulish or spiritual. What is it to be soulish? Do not think that a soulish person is a bad person. No, the best person in the world may be altogether soulish! To be soulish means to live by the soul and in the soul. To be spiritual means to live by the spirit, in the spirit, and under the direction of the spirit. This spirit is the mingled spirit: the life-giving Spirit of God mingled with our created and regenerated spirit. If we want to know the blessings and the riches in Christ, we must be in the spirit. We cannot comprehend them in the soul; we can touch them only in the spirit.

BEING BUILT UP BY GROWING
AND BEING TRANSFORMED IN SPIRIT

And I, brothers, was not able to speak to you as to spiritual men, but as to fleshy, as to infants in Christ. (1 Cor. 3:1)

Being fleshy is different from being fleshly. For example, 1 Corinthians 3 and 4 mention the problems among the Corinthians. They had jealousy, strife, and opinions; that is to be fleshly. Then chapters five and six refer to the matter of fornication among the Corinthians. There was even a brother who took his stepmother to be his wife. That is to be fleshy. You can be a civilized person with a high morality and a good reputation and yet have opinions, jealousy, and strife when you are with the brothers and sisters. This is to be fleshly. But if someone takes his stepmother to be his wife, as the brother in Corinth did, or if someone is joined to a prostitute, this kind of sin of fornication is fleshy. Some say that 1 Corinthians mentions three kinds of people. This is correct. Strictly speaking, however, 1 Corinthians mentions four kinds of people: the spiritual, the soulish, the fleshly, and the fleshy. Dear brothers and sisters, the Corinthians received so many gifts, yet the gifts could not make them spiritual. According to the New Testament, the church that had the most tongue-speaking was the church in Corinth, yet the church in Corinth was not only fleshly but also fleshy. This should be a warning to us.

You are God's cultivated land, God's building. (3:9)

Cultivated land needs to grow crops, and a building needs to be built. Growth and building are connected here because we are not a dead house but a living house. Strictly speaking, we are not built together; rather, we grow together. The real building of the church comes from growth.

> According to the grace of God given to me, as a wise master builder I have laid a foundation, and another builds upon it. But let each man take heed how he builds upon it. (v. 10)

> Do you not know that you are the temple of God, and that the Spirit of God dwells in you? If anyone destroys the temple of God, God will destroy him; for the temple of God is holy, and such are you. (vv. 16-17)

After reading all these verses, we can see that 1 Corinthians chapter one is on Christ, chapter two is on the Spirit, and chapter three is on the building. First, Christ is presented to us, then we need to experience Christ in the Spirit, and the issue is for the building. This Spirit is the Spirit who dwells in the temple of God, and He is also the building Spirit. How does God's building come about? First, the Holy Spirit who is in us causes us to grow. It is "God who causes the growth" (v. 7), and this reference to God refers to the Holy Spirit. We are God's farm, God's building. When we have the growth, we have the building. Second, the Holy Spirit who is in us is transforming us. The materials used here are gold, silver, and precious stones, not wood, grass, and stubble. However, in our nature we are not gold, silver, or precious stones; instead, we all are clay. How can we become gold, silver, and precious stones? To be sure, there is the need for transformation. This is why 1 Corinthians is followed by 2 Corinthians. The first book is on building and the second book is on transformation.

God has given Christ to us and has put us in Christ so that Christ may be our portion and our all. This can become reality only in the spirit. When we experience Christ in spirit, on the one hand, we grow, and on the other hand, we are transformed. In chapter two you can see the fact of transformation. At the end of chapter two, it says that we have the mind of Christ. Formerly, our mind was void of Christ, but now our mind, having been transformed, is filled with Christ.

We have been transformed by the renewing of our mind, as referred to in Romans 12:2. Romans 12 also shows us that the coordination in the Body and the building of the church depend on the transformation by the renewing of the mind, which is the transformation of the soul. The mind is the main part of the soul. Hence, the transformation of the mind represents the transformation of every part of the soul. Only in this transformation can there be the coordination and the building.

In chapter three we cannot find the word *transformation,* but we can see the fact of transformation. The materials for building are gold, silver, and precious stones, yet our natural being is everything other than gold, silver, and precious stones. Hence, we need transformation. Where does this transformation come from? It comes altogether from the indwelling Spirit, the Spirit who dwells in us as the temple of God. This Spirit is the building Spirit, and the way He builds is, first, by causing us to grow, and second, by transforming us. In Matthew 13 the Lord spoke six parables which are related to the church. The first one is on sowing, the second is on the tares, the third is on the mustard seed, and the fourth is on the meal that came out of wheat to form the bread. These four parables, which all refer to farm products, involve growth. Then they are followed by two parables that involve transformation: one concerning the treasure hidden in the field and the other concerning the pearl produced in the waters of the sea. In these parables, the first group shows that the farm products need growth, and the latter group shows that the building materials need transformation. As we are growing and being transformed, we become building materials. It is here that we are being built up together for the Holy Spirit to dwell among us.

But he who is joined to the Lord is one spirit. (1 Cor. 6:17)

This is a tremendously great verse. I suggest that you highlight this verse with a striking color. The last Adam became a life-giving Spirit, and this life-giving Spirit came into us and made us one spirit with Him.

Or do you not know that your body is a temple of the Holy Spirit within you, whom you have from God, and you are not your own? For you have been bought with a price. So then glorify God in your body. (vv. 19-20)

What does it mean to "glorify God in your body"? We must remember that Romans 12 says that we should present our bodies a living sacrifice to live the Body life. Hence, "to glorify God in your body" means, on the one hand, that you are joined to the Lord, and on the other hand, that you need to live the Body life. You have to realize that the spirit within you is joined to the Lord as one spirit, and therefore your body must be used by this spirit. The result of your body being used by the spirit is that your body is for the Body of Christ. In this way you glorify God in your body. In your body is this spirit, and this spirit is the spirit that is joined to the Lord's Spirit as one spirit. Therefore, your body should not be used by anything other than the spirit. When your body is used by the spirit, the result is that you are joined to the Lord's Body as one. This is to glorify God in your body, and this is also to be built together with all the saints from the spirit inwardly to the body outwardly. Here again you see the concept, the thought, of building.

> But she is more blessed if she so remains, according to my opinion; but I think that I also have the Spirit of God. (7:40)

This word is very meaningful.

> And all were baptized unto Moses in the cloud and in the sea; and all ate the same spiritual food, and all drank the same spiritual drink; for they drank of a spiritual rock which followed them, and the rock was Christ. (10:2-4)

These verses give us a principle. What we Christians eat, drink, and depend upon should all be in spirit. What you eat is spiritual food, what you drink is spiritual drink, and what you depend upon is a spiritual rock. Everything is in spirit, and even your enjoyment of Christ must be in spirit.

> For also in one Spirit we were all baptized into one Body, whether Jews or Greeks, whether slaves or free, and were all given to drink one Spirit. (12:13)

When you are baptized in the Spirit, you get into the Spirit, just as when you are baptized, you get into the water.

When you drink of one Spirit, the Spirit gets into you, just as when you drink water, water gets into you. This is one matter with two sides; furthermore, you see a sequence here. The outward baptism is for the inward drinking. First we are baptized in one Spirit and then we drink one Spirit; first we have the baptism in the Spirit outwardly and then we can drink one Spirit inwardly.

A SPIRITUAL MAN BEING EVEN MORE HUMAN

Up to this point, the message on 1 Corinthians may be considered completed. Chapter seven shows us that such a one who lives in the spirit is not so clear that he is in the spirit. The more spiritual a person is and the more he lives in the spirit, he is less clear and less conscious that he is in the spirit. This is the case in 1 Corinthians 7, where Paul said concerning marriage, "I charge, not I but the Lord" (v. 10); "I say, I, not the Lord" (v. 12). In effect, he was saying, "This is my word, not the Lord's." However, after saying so much, eventually he said, "She is more blessed if she so remains, according to my opinion; but I think that I also have the Spirit of God" (v. 40). This shows that the more a person lives in spirit, he is not so clear in his feeling that he is living in spirit. When someone says to you, "I am absolutely in spirit," you have to put a big question mark on his word. He is probably mostly in the soul. He does not have the fact of being in spirit; he only has the feeling of the soul. If you read 1 Corinthians 7 again, you will see that the more a person lives in spirit, the more human he is in his living, doing, and speaking. We have a mistaken concept in thinking that if a person lives in spirit, he will be almost like an angel and be different from human beings. This is wrong. When you read the Epistles written by Paul, you can see that he spoke one hundred percent as a man. He did not say that he had the assurance that his speaking was in the spirit. The more spiritual a person is, the less angelic he is. The more spiritual a person is, the more human he is.

I can never forget the word I heard from Brother Watchman Nee over thirty years ago. He said, "Brother, do you know that if we dress ourselves in a less sophisticated way, we will have a greater impact? And if we dress ourselves in an uncommon and 'peculiar' manner and then give a spiritual message, people will be more inclined to follow us?" Previously I did not understand this word, but now I understand it. I realize that people have a strange notion, thinking that if someone is spiritual, he or she is no longer human. This concept is not according to the truth. When the Lord Jesus was incarnated, He became a man, not an angel. He ate, slept, and put on clothes just like a man. He was truly a man. Therefore, brothers, learn not to pretend or imitate. Do not act in a certain way to make others think that you are spiritual. Real spirituality is lived out from the new man within you, while outwardly you are still very human.

DRINKING THE SPIRIT MOMENT BY MOMENT

Chapter ten tells us that our spiritual enjoyment, spiritual food, spiritual drink, and spiritual dependence all should be in the spirit. Chapter twelve speaks even more thoroughly. On the one hand, we have been baptized in one Spirit, and on the other hand, we are drinking of one Spirit day by day. Baptism is a matter that is once for all, but drinking just once is not enough. We must drink daily. Therefore, although we need the proper outpouring of the Spirit, the outward pouring out is for the inward receiving and taking in. Instead of asking for the outpouring of the Spirit day by day, we should receive, take in, the Spirit from within moment by moment.

Let us refer again to the matter of speaking in tongues in the Pentecostal movement. Those who are in the Pentecostal movement care for nothing but speaking in tongues, but little do they know that speaking in tongues is not drinking of the Holy Spirit. A donkey in the Old Testament also spoke in tongues, yet it did not drink one bit of the Holy Spirit. Even if the speaking in tongues is genuine, at most it is an outpouring. First Corinthians 12:13 clearly shows us that the outward pouring and the inward drinking are two different matters. God has baptized us into the Spirit, and from then on He also has made us to drink of the Spirit. God has baptized us into the Spirit as the living water, and He has also made us to drink of this living water. The Pentecostal movement gives people only a one-sided impression, causing people to care for the outward aspect and altogether neglect the inward aspect. Today God desires to have a great recovery, the recovery of the inward drinking of the Spirit.

The last Adam became a life-giving Spirit. (15:45)

Finally, chapter fifteen shows that Christ in resurrection is the life-giving Spirit. The Spirit who dwells in us, who causes us to grow and be transformed, and who is building us into the temple of God, as mentioned in chapter three, is this life-giving Spirit. The Spirit in us to whom we are joined, as mentioned in chapter six, is also this life-giving Spirit. Furthermore, the Spirit who dwells in our body to make our body exclusively for His use is also this life-giving Spirit. This Spirit is Christ Himself as our portion. We should eat Him as our spiritual food, drink Him as our spiritual drink, and depend upon Him as our spiritual rock. Every day we are drinking of this one Spirit to receive His supply. This is the book of 1 Corinthians.

Finally, we have a word of conclusion. Following the book of Romans, 1 Corinthians shows us that God has given Christ to us to be our portion and our everything. This Christ must be the life-giving Spirit in our spirit. Only by this can we enjoy Him practically, and only by this can He become our real experience. When we experience Him in this way, we grow and are transformed so that we are built up together to be the temple of God. Then the Spirit can dwell among us. Moreover, when you live in this Spirit, you become very human, and you may not even feel very much that you are in the spirit. When you live in the spirit in a deep way, you may not have such a strong feeling about it. This, however, is the normal condition.

CHAPTER FOUR

SECOND CORINTHIANS

But the One who firmly attaches us with you unto Christ and has anointed us is God, He who has also sealed us and given the Spirit in our hearts as a pledge. (2 Cor. 1:21-22)

Since you are being manifested that you are a letter of Christ ministered by us, inscribed not with ink but with the Spirit of the living God; not in tablets of stone but in tablets of hearts of flesh. (3:3)

Who has also made us sufficient as ministers of a new covenant, ministers not of the letter but of the Spirit; for the letter kills, but the Spirit gives life. (v. 6)

And the Lord is the Spirit; and where the Spirit of the Lord is, there is freedom. But we all with unveiled face, beholding and reflecting like a mirror the glory of the Lord, are being transformed into the same image from glory to glory, even as from the Lord Spirit. (vv. 17-18)

For the weapons of our warfare are not fleshly but powerful before God for the overthrowing of strongholds, as we overthrow reasonings and every high thing rising up against the knowledge of God, and take captive every thought unto the obedience of Christ. (10:4-5)

Test yourselves whether you are in the faith; prove yourselves. Or do you not realize about yourselves that Jesus Christ is in you, unless you are disapproved? (13:5)

The grace of the Lord Jesus Christ and the love of God and the fellowship of the Holy Spirit be with you all. (v. 14)

First Corinthians shows us the building Spirit. The primary need for building is transformation. Therefore, 2 Corinthians goes on to show us the transforming Spirit. The Spirit in 2 Corinthians is the transforming Spirit.

ANOINTING, SEALING, AND PLEDGING

Second Corinthians 1 shows that the transforming Spirit is in us as three items doing three things. First, He is the ointment to anoint us; second, He is the seal to impress us; and third, He is the pledge to guarantee to us. These three matters alone require us to have much knowledge, explanation, and experience.

The first portion in the Bible that mentions the anointing of the Spirit who dwells in us is 2 Corinthians 1. As the ointment, the Spirit anoints us and "rubs" God's elements into us. When you apply any kind of ointment to an object, the more you apply, the more the element of the ointment is added to the object. The life-giving Spirit works within us, and the first thing He does is to rub God's elements into us. His anointing within is His moving, and this moving is a rubbing to apply the divine elements into us.

Second, the Spirit is the seal. This is for us to have God's image. A seal is a matter of image. If your seal is square, the impression it makes will also be square. If your seal is round, the impression it makes will also be round. As the seal in us, the life-giving Spirit not only affirms that we belong to God but also impresses God's image into us so that we have God's image. Let us give an example. Sometimes we meet someone in a train, in a steamboat, or in other situations. Although we do not know that person, by his or her appearance we know that this one is a brother or a sister. That appearance is the impression of the seal. This seal is living and is a reality. When we truly live in the Spirit and walk according to the Spirit, wherever we are we have a kind of image, a kind of impression, a kind of appearance, by which others can recognize that we belong to God.

Third, the Spirit is the pledge. In Greek, this word has many denotations. It may be translated as *evidence, pledge, guarantee, deposit, earnest, sample,* or *foretaste.* This Spirit as the ointment in us anoints us with God's elements, and as the seal He impresses us with the image of God, affirming that we belong to God and have God's image. Furthermore, as the pledge, He guarantees that all the fullness of the Godhead is our portion for our enjoyment and application. This Spirit enables us to have a foretaste of God, to enjoy God in advance.

INSCRIBING, MINISTERING, AND FREEING

Now we come to 2 Corinthians 3. This chapter first shows that this Spirit who is in us as the anointing, the sealing, and the pledging is also the inscribing Spirit. We are like a piece of paper, and the Spirit of life is like ink, with which Christ is inscribed into us. This thought is deep and meaningful.

Many different expressions are used in the Epistles to describe the indwelling Spirit. Some of the titles are found in Romans, while other expressions are found in 1 Corinthians. Now in 2 Corinthians there are still more utterances. In Romans and 1 Corinthians there are no words referring to the anointing, the sealing, the pledging, or the inscribing. Then 2 Corinthians 3 shows that the Spirit is the inscribing Spirit (v. 3) and the Spirit who gives life (v. 6). Moreover, verse 8 of the same chapter mentions "the ministry of the Spirit." Therefore, the Spirit is also the ministering Spirit. This ministering Spirit is the Spirit of life, the writing or inscribing Spirit. By this you can see that just chapter three of 2 Corinthians alone has added a number of different expressions.

We have said before that the first thing in the degradation of the church on earth is that the replacements of Christ were brought in, and the next thing is that man's will, organization, and methods have replaced the Holy Spirit. You see here, however, that the Holy Spirit is the inscribing Spirit. What does He inscribe? The Spirit inscribes Christ. Paul said, "You are being manifested that you are a letter of Christ" (v. 3a). This letter speaks about Christ. Whatever is written in this letter is Christ. This tells us that today when we help others, whether it is to preach the word, to give a message, to preach the gospel, or to visit and fellowship with others, what we are doing is to write Christ into others through the Spirit. This is to work Christ into others, to minister Christ into others. You do not merely preach to people a message about Christ; rather, you work Christ into them.

This requires you to exercise your spirit. You cannot

minister Christ merely by doctrines or theories. You must be in spirit in order to touch the spirit in man's deepest part. It is neither a matter of how many messages you preach concerning Christ nor a matter of how many things you speak about Christ. Rather, it is a matter of the exercise of the spirit, the release of the spirit, and the going forth of the spirit. It is better that we give fewer messages. Our spirit must be strong, rich, living, and full of supply. When our spirit goes forth, it touches others' spirit. What this spirit does in others is to write Christ into them.

The conclusion of 2 Corinthians 3 tells us that the Spirit is the Lord Himself. Moreover, it says that where the Spirit is, there is release, there is freedom. Therefore, the Spirit is also the freeing Spirit, the Spirit who sets us free. Then it goes on to say that this Spirit is also the transforming Spirit. The latter part of verse 18 says, "Being transformed...even as from the Lord Spirit." The same word for *transformed* is also used in Romans 12:2, which says, "Be transformed by the renewing of the mind." Therefore, in 2 Corinthians the Spirit is the anointing, the sealing, and the pledging, and He is also the inscribing Spirit, the ministering Spirit, the Spirit who gives life, the freeing Spirit, and the transforming Spirit. The utterance here is truly rich. I have a strong feeling that today we do not have adequate knowledge of the Spirit. I hope that in these days the Lord will cause us to see that the most important thing in following the Lord is to know the Spirit. We ourselves must have the experience, and then we have to preach and teach about this Spirit, showing others how this Spirit inwardly anoints us, rubbing God's elements into us. We should describe to them how this Spirit seals us, not once for all but continuously, so that the more He seals us, the more we become like God, the more we have God's image. We should also illustrate to them how the Spirit is in us as the foretaste, sample, and earnest, guaranteeing that everything of God is for our enjoyment. We should also explain to them that the Spirit is inscribing Christ in us daily. Hence, today when we help others, whether in ministering the word, in preaching the gospel, in fellowshipping, or in visiting, we should exercise our spirit to let the Spirit inscribe, add, work, and minister more of Christ into them. Furthermore, we should explain to them how the Spirit enlivens us from within and gives us life. We should show them that our service, our ministering, and our ministry should issue out of the Spirit. We should also show them how the Spirit releases us, because where the Spirit is, there is freedom; He has loosed all confinements, bondage, and restraints so that we are liberated, transcended, uplifted, and ascended. We should also illustrate to others how the Spirit is doing a transforming work in us daily and how we need to open our mind, our heart, our spirit, and even our entire being to afford Him the opportunity to flow in us and carry out His transforming work. The more He transforms us, the more we bear His image.

THE TRANSFORMING SPIRIT

Romans leads us to see the Body, whereas 1 Corinthians shows us that the Body needs to be built, that the Spirit within us is the building Spirit, and that the basic need for the building is transformation. This matter has been referred to in 1 Corinthians and even in Romans, but it is mentioned most clearly in 2 Corinthians. When the Holy Spirit comes into us, we are regenerated. Regeneration is a matter of the spirit. However, transformation is not a matter of the spirit. Romans 12 shows us that transformation begins with our mind; our mind is first renewed and then transformed. Our mind is the leading part of our soul. When our mind is transformed, our emotion and will also are transformed. We all have been saved and regenerated, and there is no problem with this. However, regeneration is a matter that is in our spirit. Our problem now is not with regeneration but with transformation. Some of us may be more transformed, some may be less transformed, and some may not be transformed at all.

The anointing of the Spirit in us is for our transformation. The sealing of the Spirit to impress us with the image of God is for our transformation. The Spirit as the pledge in us and as the firstfruit for our enjoyment and foretaste is for our transformation. He is inscribing a letter to write Christ in us for our transformation. He is the ministering Spirit to loose us and to free us, which is also for our transformation. Transformation simply means that we allow the Spirit of life who indwells us to saturate our spirit and spread outward to permeate our mind, emotion, and will.

Brothers and sisters, please remember that transformation is absolutely related to building. Consider this: Can three brothers who are regenerated but have not been transformed be built together? No, they cannot. Why? Their soul is a hindrance. They are regenerated in their spirit, but they have different views, ideas, preferences, and decisions. Thus, how can they be built together? Therefore, brothers, building depends not on man's work but on transformation. If a brother has been transformed and his mind, emotion, and will have been saturated with the Spirit, it is very easy for him to coordinate and be built together with another brother who also has been transformed. Thank the Lord, depending on how much transformation there is, that is how much building there will be.

Several young brothers and sisters went to the United States and were there for a few years. Originally they were very useful in the different localities in Asia, but after they went to America, they were not able to manifest their usefulness. One time when I was with them, they asked, "Brother Lee, why is it that we cannot manifest our usefulness here? It seems that we have become unemployed." I said, "This matter is very mysterious, but do you know that on the whole earth the people who are the hardest to be broken are the Chinese? Their national characteristic is too conservative. On the one hand, this kind of national characteristic is quite good, but on the other hand, it is a great hindrance that prevents the Lord from coming out of us. Look at the people who come from Europe, Australia, South America, and Africa. After they have been in America for one or two generations, they look just like Americans. However, the Chinese, after being in America three or four generations, are still full of the Chinese "smell"; they have not changed at all. After living in America all these years, you have not changed a bit but have remained Chinese brothers and Chinese sisters. You expect every brother and sister to be like you before you can serve and minister to them. Therefore, in order for the Lord to come out from you, firstly, you as Chinese people must be broken and transformed. Yes, you have a spirit, yet you do not live by the spirit. Rather, you live by your mind and emotion. Your mind is a stronghold that locks the Lord securely within you so that He cannot break through. Chinese habits, Chinese concepts, Chinese thoughts, and Chinese mentality all are in the mind. This stronghold must be overthrown."

Dear brothers and sisters, your problem today is that you are often in your mind. You are under a cloud of theories. The more you are in the theories, the more confused your mind is. However, if you are willing to forsake your mind and return to your spirit, everything will be clear. Do you remember Psalm 73:16-17? There the psalmist said that when he considered the matter in order to understand it, it was a troublesome task in his sight, but when he went into the sanctuary of God, the matter became clear. You say you are not clear about this matter or that matter; this is because you are in your mind. Once you come back to your spirit, you will be clear.

Therefore, the basic need for the coordination and building is transformation. You should let Christ swallow up everything. You should never excuse yourself. Not one excuse is valid. Others may excuse you, but you should not excuse yourself. You should allow Christ to have the ground in you and come out of you so that you may be gradually transformed. Your body is not a problem; the problem is all in your soul. Today the problem in the church is that our mentality, our emotion, and our will are troublesome. The problems of the brothers and sisters, as well as the problems of the church, all arise out of the mind, emotion, and will.

God's redemption consists of three steps: regeneration in the spirit, transformation in the soul, and transfiguration in the body. We have already received regeneration in our spirit as the first step, we will have the transfiguration of our body as our portion in the future, and now we are in the process of being transformed in our soul. What God is doing today is the work of transformation. How does He do it? By the Holy Spirit's anointing, sealing, supplying, inscribing, and releasing in us to saturate every part of our soul with Christ. Thus, every part of our soul will be transformed. You will be transformed, I will be transformed, and we all will be transformed. We will be one in spirit and one in soul. In this way we will be built together.

Philippians 1:27 says, "You stand firm in one spirit, with one soul striving together along with the faith of the gospel." To serve in one spirit with one soul is to be in oneness. The brothers and sisters are usually one in spirit. It is their soul that is mischievous, troublesome, disturbing, and bothersome. Your mind, your emotion, and your will are giving you trouble. Hence, you must return to the spirit, remain in the spirit, and let the spirit subdue your soul. When the spirit conquers your mind, your mind is changed. The spirit is connected to the Lord. When you are in subjection to the spirit, you are in subjection to the Lord. However, some brothers and sisters are not like this. They do not care about the spirit; they care only for their emotions. When their emotions are troubled, they say, "I cannot take it; I don't care. I will do this and I will do that." When they are not able to take it and when they do not care, they become a trouble in the church.

Dear brothers and sisters, there are so many people and so many matters in the church. In such a complicated situation, how can everything be according to your feeling and fit the taste of your emotions? This is impossible. If you learn the lesson and know the Lord, and if you turn to your spirit, even if there are a million things, none will affect or influence you. This is because you are in the spirit. Instead of listening to your emotion, you listen to your spirit. The emotion is affected by the circumstance, but the spirit is under the direction of the Lord. If you live in the emotion, you will surely be touched by the environment, but if you live in the spirit, your spirit will be so strong that it dominates your emotion. No matter how the circumstance fluctuates, you remain the same in spirit.

Therefore, the coordination in the church is a matter of the spirit. The solution to the problems of the church is also a matter of the spirit. We have our reason, but everyone has a reason; even the thieves have their reasons. No one admits that he is wrong. Therefore, it is not a matter of right or wrong, nor is it a matter of likes or dislikes, but a matter of returning to the spirit. As long as we are in the spirit, and as the spirit spreads outward to saturate our entire soul, then in this one spirit with one soul we are built together.

THE SOUL-LIFE BEING CONSUMED AND THE FACULTIES OF THE SOUL BEING RENEWED

Following chapter three of 2 Corinthians, chapter four says that there is a treasure in earthen vessels. Earthen vessels need to be broken, changed in nature, and transformed. Although the outer man is being consumed, the inner man is being renewed day by day. What is the outer man, and what is the inner man? With the outer man, the soul is the life and the body is the instrument. With the inner man, the spirit is the life and the soul is the instrument. The man who takes the soul as the life and the body as the instrument needs to be consumed day by day. The man who takes the spirit as the life and the faculties of the soul as the instrument needs to be renewed day by day. This means that the spirit is so strengthened that it saturates every part of the soul. When the soul-life is put to death, the faculties of the soul are more and more renewed and uplifted. In the outer man there is the element of the soul, and in the inner man there is also the element of the soul. However, in the outer man the soul is the life, whereas in the inner man the soul with its faculties is the instrument. To put the soul to death is not to put its faculties to death but to put its life to death. To renew the soul is not to renew its life but to renew its faculties. The soul-life must be put to death, while the faculties of the soul must be renewed, uplifted, and broadened. After the renewing of the soul, your mind will become more useful because it will be a renewed, uplifted, and broadened mind. Any faculty that belongs to the flesh, to sin, or to the soul must be consumed, but the spirit as life and the faculties of the soul must be renewed, transformed, and strengthened day by day. This is the work of the transforming Spirit in us.

GRACE, LOVE, AND FELLOWSHIP

Verse 5 of chapter thirteen is a special charge to show that Christ is in us. If we have faith, we are not disapproved because we have Christ in us. This Christ who is in us is the Spirit.

Finally, at the conclusion of this book, the apostle gives a blessing with these words: "The grace of the Lord Jesus Christ and the love of God and the fellowship of the Holy Spirit be with you all." The Lord Jesus, God, and the Holy Spirit are triune, and grace, love, and fellowship are also triune.

Why is grace mentioned first instead of love? Because the goal, the central concept, is Christ as grace. In chapter twelve the apostle said that there was a thorn in his flesh for which he entreated the Lord three times that it might depart from him, but the Lord said to him, "My grace is sufficient for you" (v. 9). The main purpose of this book is for us to experience the Lord as grace. The source of this grace is the love of God, and the transmission of this grace is the fellowship of the Holy Spirit. Love, grace, and fellowship are all one thing. Love is the source of grace, grace is the expression of love, and through fellowship grace is transmitted to us. This may be compared to the electrical source, the electrical current, and the electricity itself being three-in-one. The source of electricity is electricity, the current of electricity is electricity, and electricity itself is electricity. But without these three aspects of electricity, the electricity cannot come into the room. There is a place where the electricity is generated, and that is the electrical source. There is the electrical current that is transmitted to us, and there is also the electricity itself. In our explanation it seems that there are different aspects of the electricity, but actually the electrical source is the electricity itself, the electrical current is also the electricity, and the substance of electricity is still the electricity itself. Likewise, love, which is in the Father, is the source. Grace, which is in the Son, is the expression. And fellowship, which is through the Holy Spirit, is the transmission. This is one matter with three aspects. The Father is the source, Christ is the expression, and the Holy Spirit is the transmission. The Holy Spirit transmits what the Son is and what the Father has into us. This is the work of the Spirit of life. Hence, at the end of 2 Corinthians, the apostle concludes by saying, "The grace of the Lord Jesus Christ and the love of God and the fellowship of the Holy Spirit be with you all." When the Holy Spirit flows within us, the grace of Christ becomes our enjoyment. What we need today is to experience, enjoy, and know this matter.

Dear brothers and sisters, these are the "stories" in the Spirit. We all must know this Spirit and know how to come back to our spirit to contact the life-giving Spirit, the all-inclusive Spirit, who is the rich Christ, that we may enjoy all the fullness of God.

GALATIANS

Now we come to the book of Galatians. The sequence of the books of the Bible is very meaningful, and we believe it is the arrangement of the Holy Spirit. In Romans we see how the Spirit of sonship carries out a sanctifying work in us so that we may have the image of God's Son. Then 1 Corinthians tells us how this Spirit is building us. The building Spirit carries out a building work in us mainly by transforming us. Therefore, 2 Corinthians goes on to show how the transforming Spirit is doing a transforming work in us. This is a general outline. Then from Galatians to Philemon we see a more detailed explanation of how we can become sons of God, how the Son of God can be wrought into us, how we can live by the Son of God, and how we can become the Body of Christ, thus completely living in the life-giving Spirit.

It pleased God...to reveal His Son in me. (Gal. 1:15-16)

The first concept given to us in Galatians is that it pleased God to reveal His Son in us, to put His Son in us.

For I through law have died to law that I might live to God. I am crucified with Christ; and it is no longer I who live, but it is Christ who lives in me; and the life which I now live in the flesh I live in faith, the faith of the Son of God, who loved me and gave Himself up for me. (2:19-20)

What these two verses mean is that the Son of God is in me, the faith of the Son of God is in me, and I live by the faith of the Son of God. Chapter one says it pleases God to put His Son in us. Chapter two says the Son of God has not only been put in us, but He is also living in us, and we are living by His faith.

My children, with whom I travail again in birth until Christ
is formed in you. (4:19)

The above three passages are the basic thoughts in the
book of Galatians. First, the Son of God is revealed in us and
is put in us. Second, the Son of God lives in us. Third, the Son
of God is being formed in us. Being put in us is the first step,
living in us is the continuation, and being formed in us is
the result. How is this matter being accomplished? It is altogether accomplished in the Spirit.

But just as at that time he who was born according to the
flesh persecuted him who was born according to the Spirit, so
also it is now. (v. 29)

Here we have the matter of being born according to the
Spirit, which means the same thing as being born of the Spirit
in John 3.

But when the fullness of the time came, God sent forth His
Son, born of a woman, born under law, that He might redeem
those under law that we might receive the sonship. And because you are sons, God has sent forth the Spirit of His Son
into our hearts, crying, Abba, Father! (Gal. 4:4-6)

The gospel preached in Christianity always contains an
inaccurate concept, that is, that Christ has redeemed us out
of the law for us to enjoy the blessing of heaven. However,
Galatians 4 does not say this. Instead, it says that God has
redeemed us out of the law that we may receive the sonship.
The central purpose of Christ's redemption is not for us to
enjoy the blessing of going to heaven but for us to receive the
sonship and become sons of God. Furthermore, the Spirit of
the Son here is somewhat different from the Spirit of sonship
in Romans 8. Here it is the Spirit of Christ as the Son of God.
Whereas Galatians 4:29 says, "Born according to the Spirit,"
here in 4:6 it says that God has sent "the Spirit of His Son"
into our hearts.

This only I wish to learn from you, Did you receive the Spirit
out of the works of law or out of the hearing of faith? Are you
so foolish? Having begun by the Spirit, are you now being
perfected by the flesh? (3:2-3)

He therefore who bountifully supplies to you the Spirit and

does works of power among you, does He do it out of the works of law or out of the hearing of faith? (v. 5)

And the Scripture, foreseeing that God would justify the Gentiles out of faith, announced the gospel beforehand to Abraham: "In you shall all the nations be blessed." (v. 8)

Christ has redeemed us out of the curse of the law, having become a curse on our behalf; because it is written, "Cursed is every one hanging on a tree"; in order that the blessing of Abraham might come to the Gentiles in Christ Jesus, that we might receive the promise of the Spirit through faith. (vv. 13-14)

The blessing which God intended to give to Abraham was the promise of the Spirit. Many Christians do not see this. They think that the gospel is for the forgiveness of sins, which surely is a blessing. In the Gospels, however, the principal blessing is the life-giving Spirit whom God intended to give us according to what He had planned and ordained in eternity. Therefore, in time, God promised Abraham, saying that in his seed, who is Christ, all the nations would be blessed.

I have never read a spiritual book or heard a message saying that this blessing is the life-giving Spirit. It was not until over ten years ago, one morning when I came to this passage in my studying of the Bible, my eyes were opened by God to see that this blessing is the promise of the Spirit. This Spirit comprises the Father, the Son, and the Spirit. Not only so, this Spirit also includes the human element, the effectiveness of Christ's death, and the power of resurrection. This Spirit is truly the all-inclusive Spirit.

Many Christians consider the Holy Spirit to be very simple. There were even theological debates on whether or not the Holy Spirit is a person. In the early days, the general concept was that the Holy Spirit was merely a power, an agent. Later, advancement in theology led to the discovery of the Holy Spirit as a person. Today we must see that the Holy Spirit is not only a person, but that He also incorporates the Father and the Son. Moreover, He is all-inclusive. He has the elements of human living, the effectiveness of death, and the power of resurrection. The Spirit, therefore, is exceedingly rich.

Galatians 3:5 shows that God is supplying, not just

giving, the Spirit to us. To supply means to meet our need continuously. God not only gives us the Holy Spirit; He supplies to us the Holy Spirit. This Spirit is the blessing which God planned and prepared throughout the ages for us. When you have this Spirit, you have eternal life. When you have this Spirit, you have redemption. Comfort, peace, and power all are in this Spirit. Do not misunderstand me, but even forgiveness of sins is in this Spirit.

I hope that here I can give you a simple yet deep impression. This Spirit is a tremendous Spirit. All that God is and all that Christ has accomplished, obtained, and attained are in this Spirit. When we believe the gospel, God puts this Spirit into us. When this Spirit comes in, forgiveness of sins, redemption, justification, peace, life, comfort, power, and light come in. The Father, the Son, and the Spirit come in, and even the effectiveness of the death of Christ, which solves all our problems, and the power of resurrection come in. Hence, this is an all-effective dose. He can handle your every problem and supply your every need.

DYING TO THE LAW
THAT CHRIST MAY BE FORMED IN US

The apostle wrote the book of Galatians with a strong intention to break down the Galatians' concept of keeping the law. The problem of the Galatians is the problem of every Christian. According to our natural concept, we the saved ones all have a desire to do good. In other words, we like to keep the law. Immediately after we are saved, we have a concept within us, thinking that before we believed in the Lord, we had a bad temper and our conduct was poor; now that we are saved, we ought to improve our conduct and behave properly. The strange thing is that every Christian has this concept also whenever he is revived. He has the feeling that formerly he was a careless and indifferent Christian, but now since he has been revived through the Lord's mercy, he should behave properly and not be so loose.

Brothers and sisters, is this concept right or wrong? Humanly speaking, it is a very good concept; from God's viewpoint, however, it is wrong. This kind of doing good is equivalent to the Jews' keeping of the law. It is the flesh that keeps the law and works out the law. Whenever man desires to do good, he uses his own strength. Sometimes you know that you are weak, so you pray to the Lord for help. However, the Lord will never answer this kind of prayer. Truthfully speaking, the more you wish to do good, the more the Lord wishes that you would not do good. You think that it would be good if you could succeed, but the Lord considers that it would be good if you fail. For example, you may have a bad temper, so you pray to the Lord, asking Him to help you to be patient. However, the more you pray in this way, the less patience you have. Your temper worsens, even to such an extent that you are altogether disappointed with yourself. You say, "Lord, I have no way anymore!" When such a day comes, the Lord would say, "This is wonderful!" Why? Because His intention is not for us to do good.

Brothers and sisters, God has no intention for us to do good. Rather, God wants us to live out Christ. God's goal is not the law but Christ. Galatians chapter one says it pleased God to reveal His Son in us. Chapter two says it is no longer we who live, but it is Christ who lives in us. It is not we who are doing good, but it is Christ who lives in us.

Man was created in the image of God, and the image of God is Christ. Second Corinthians 4:4 says that Christ is the image of God. Colossians 1:15 also says that the beloved Son is the image of God. Why did God create man according to Christ? He did this in order that one day He might put Christ in man. Man is a vessel to contain Christ. A glove is made according to the shape of the hand, and it is also made to contain the hand. If I want to put my hand into the glove, but the glove is uncooperative and does not give me the room, my hand cannot be comfortable inside the glove. All the fingers of my hand must fit into the glove; only then can my hand feel comfortable. At that moment the glove is altogether the same as the shape of the hand. We may say that the hand has been formed in the glove.

After we have been saved, the Lord Jesus is in us. However, He is very frustrated in us, and sometimes He is imprisoned in our spirit. We may not give Him any ground in our soul, including our mind, emotion, and will. Finally one day, as we are moved by His love, we gradually open ourselves to Him and give Him more ground. Then He is able to spread outward. At a certain time we may have an argument with the Lord again, and we are not willing to give Him more ground; then He has to stop there and wait patiently. Sometimes He may be gracious to us and may draw us with His love, yet it is still to no avail. Then He may be forced to lift His hand to give us a little blow. In any case, if you would not be subdued by Him this year, two years later He will subdue you. If you would not be subdued by Him in this life, He will subdue you when He comes back. Since He is in us, in spite of everything He must be formed in us.

WALKING BY THE SPIRIT
TO BEAR THE FRUIT OF THE SPIRIT

If we live by the Spirit, let us also walk by the Spirit. (Gal. 5:25)

But I say, Walk by the Spirit and you shall by no means fulfill the lust of the flesh. For the flesh lusts against the Spirit, and the Spirit against the flesh; for these oppose each other that you would not do the things that you desire. But if you are led by the Spirit, you are not under the law. (vv. 16-18)

But the fruit of the Spirit is love, joy, peace, long-suffering, kindness, goodness, faithfulness, meekness, self-control; against such things there is no law. (vv. 22-23)

Here the fruit of the Spirit is singular. There are not nine kinds of fruits but one kind of fruit with nine aspects.

For he who sows unto his own flesh will reap corruption of the flesh, but he who sows unto the Spirit will of the Spirit reap eternal life. (6:8)

Brothers, even if a man is overtaken in some offense, you who are spiritual restore such a one in a spirit of meekness. (v. 1)

However, brothers and sisters, how can Christ live in us? And how can He be formed in us? This is altogether a matter of the spirit and is carried out by the Spirit of life in us. We have been born of the Spirit. By this birth God caused the Spirit of His Son, the Spirit of Christ, even Christ Himself, to come into us. Since we have been born of the Spirit, we should live and walk by the Spirit. In this way we afford the Spirit the opportunity to spread from within us so that every part of our being is filled with the Spirit. Hence, Ephesians 4:23 uses the phrase *the spirit of your mind.* This means that the Spirit has entered our mind to become the Spirit in our mind. Since the mind, which is the leading part of the soul, has the Spirit, the emotion and will also will have the Spirit. In this way the Spirit is being formed in our entire being. This is altogether the story of the Spirit.

Therefore, the key to Galatians lies with walking by the Spirit. When you walk by the Spirit, you give the ground to Christ. When you walk by the Spirit, you allow Christ to possess you. When you walk by the Spirit, your inward being is given over to Christ little by little. You cannot simply say that Christ lives in us and is being formed in us; this is just a doctrinal truth. How does Christ live in you? How is He being formed in you? The subjective experience lies with the spirit in you. You must know how to follow this Spirit and how to apply this Spirit. Therefore, sometimes in Galatians this Spirit is not called the Holy Spirit but simply the Spirit, because this Spirit in us is in our spirit formed of two spirits. At this time this spirit is, on the one hand, the Holy Spirit, and on the other hand, our spirit.

The apostle said that if we live by the Spirit, let us also walk by the Spirit. As we live by the Spirit, the Spirit lives in us, and out of this Spirit comes fruit in many aspects. This fruit is Christ Himself. Nine aspects of this fruit are mentioned in Galatians. Actually, there are more than just nine aspects, but only nine aspects are listed as illustrations.

The apostle also exhorted us that since this is the case, we should learn to sow unto the Spirit. Whatever we do, we should do it unto this Spirit. Eventually, we will reap life. We do not have to wait until the future, in eternity, to enjoy eternal life. Rather, today we can reap eternal life. However, if we sow unto the flesh, we will reap corruption, which is death. The utterance of Galatians 6:8 is very similar to that of Romans 8:6.

Galatians 6:1 gives us an illustration. It says that when we try to restore a brother, we should exercise a spirit of meekness. In Greek it says that you should restore your brother "in a spirit of meekness." Hence, at this time, your mind is in the spirit, your action is in the spirit, your fellowship with the brothers and sisters is in the spirit, and even your restoration of a brother is in the spirit. As a result, you are a spiritual man.

DEALING WITH THE FLESH BY THE CROSS THAT THE SPIRIT MAY HAVE GROUND

The book of Galatians shows us, on the negative side, that we should not keep the law, that we have died to the law. On the positive side, it shows us that Christ lives in us and is being formed in us. The law is joined to the flesh, whereas Christ is joined to the Holy Spirit. Whenever you keep the law, that is in the flesh; whenever you live out Christ, that is in the Holy Spirit. Therefore, Galatians also refers to the cross. The cross is for us to deal with the flesh and live in the Holy Spirit. They who are of Christ Jesus have crucified the flesh with its passions and its lusts. This is not merely a doctrine but an experience. I have been crucified with Christ; it is no longer I who live. I have been terminated. Not only in committing sins there is no "I" and there is no ground for "I," but even in doing good there is also no "I" and there is no ground for "I." This "I" has died on the cross; this self is on the cross; this flesh is on the cross. I know the cross; the cross deals not only with the bad "I" but also with the good "I." I have been crucified with Christ. They who are of Christ have crucified the flesh.

The Lord Jesus said, "If anyone wants to come after Me, let him deny himself and take up his cross and follow Me" (Matt. 16:24). To deny the self is to put your self on the cross. Whenever your self wants to do good, you should put your self on the cross. Whenever your self tries to be patient, you should put your patient self on the cross. As long as you are willing to put your self on the cross, the Lord Jesus as the living Spirit will have the ground in you.

CHAPTER SIX

EPHESIANS

Following the book of Galatians is the book of Ephesians. The Spirit in Galatians is for us to have Christ, live by Christ, and live out Christ, or we may say, for us to have the Son of God, live by the Son of God, and live out the Son of God. We should not merely speak about Christ and the Son of God. Unless we know the Spirit and live in the Spirit, everything we say about Christ is doctrinal, not experiential. All our speakings concerning Christ must be in the Spirit. If we want to receive Christ and let Him come into us, and if we want to live out Christ, express Him, and let Him become the outward fruit, then we must have the "story" of the Spirit and be in the Spirit.

The Spirit in Galatians is for us to live by Christ and live out Christ, whereas the Spirit in Ephesians is for us to have the Body life, the church life. Many people know that Ephesians is a book on the church, the Body of Christ. Please remember, however, that the church is not a doctrine. In church history there was a group of people, the so-called Brethren, who had a great many discussions and writings concerning the church. They said that the church is heavenly, is seated with Christ in the heavenlies, and has received every spiritual blessing in the heavenlies in Christ. These truths are accurate. Yet it is a pity that they have become doctrines because their emphasis is merely on the objective aspect of the church. May I ask you, How can the fact that the church is in the heavenlies be fulfilled in you? How can you experience the spiritual blessings in the heavenlies that were given by God to the church? This requires you to live in the

Spirit. If you do not live in the Spirit, the fact that the church is in the heavenlies has nothing to do with you. There is an abundant supply of electricity in the power plant, but unless the electrical current is transmitted to your electric fan, the electricity in the power plant has nothing to do with you. Therefore, the reality of the church is not a matter of doctrine or a matter of interpretation but a matter of having the life-giving Spirit connected to your spirit. Once you live in the Spirit, you have the reality of the church, and you have the church life.

The spiritual life, the church life, and the reality of the Body all hinge on the Spirit. The key to knowing the Lord, following the Lord, fellowshipping with the Lord, contacting the Lord, having the church life, and having the reality of the Body is the Spirit. Only when you have the Spirit can you have a spiritual goal. Regrettably, many Christians have lost the goal. Some of them care only for studying the Bible and learning the doctrines, while others pay attention to rituals and ordinances. Still others want to receive a surge of power from on high, so they pray continually hoping that one day this surge of power from on high will be poured upon them. Their reasoning is based solely on the book of Acts, without caring for the other aspect revealed in the Gospel of John. The Gospel of John shows us that this power flows out from within instead of from on high. The Lord Jesus said that if anyone drinks of the water that He gives, the water will become in him a fountain of water gushing up all the time (John 4:14). He also said, "If anyone thirsts, let him come to Me and drink. He who believes into Me...out of his innermost being shall flow rivers of living water" (7:37-38). Here it does not speak of only one river but many rivers, a variety of rivers, such as the river of love, the river of patience, and the river of humility. These rivers are abundant, rich, and multifaceted.

There are two brothers with us in these meetings who are from America, and both of them are Texans. The western part of Texas, where one of the brother's hometown is, is famous in the world for its cotton production. I have been to his hometown for a short stay. The place is a vast plain spreading out beyond the horizon with cotton fields everywhere. I asked them about a little shed that was built in the field and was told that it is used for irrigation equipment. I learned that underneath there is a subterranean river flowing wide and deep, so the people dug a deep well to draw the water up to irrigate the region. Therefore, the cotton fields there do not depend on the rain from heaven, yet they have an abundant harvest yearly because they never lack water.

Oh, brothers and sisters, there is also a river flowing richly within us Christians, yet we neglect it and are ignorant of it. We forget that when the Lord Jesus was resurrected, He breathed into the disciples. Then at the end of the New Testament, it is still John's message that shows us a river of water of life proceeding from the throne. If anyone drinks of this water, the water will become in him a fountain flowing continuously. If this water cannot flow out, it is not because the river has no water, but because it has been shut up. The Lord Jesus is already in you, but if you do not open to Him, He cannot flow freely. Dear brothers and sisters, if you say that prayer is the secret of power, then let me tell you that the secret of prayer is to dig the well so that your inner being will be opened through prayer. The more you pray, the deeper your digging is, and the result is that the living water within you will flow out.

THE SEALING AND PLEDGING SPIRIT

There are nine main points concerning the Spirit covered in the entire book of Ephesians. The first main point gives us the overall subject matter.

> In whom you also, having heard the word of the truth, the gospel of your salvation, in Him also believing, you were sealed with the Holy Spirit of the promise, who is the pledge of our inheritance unto the redemption of the acquired possession, to the praise of His glory. (Eph. 1:13-14)

Here *the Holy Spirit* is a noun with a particular construction in Greek. The word *Holy* is a particularly emphasized word, which is impossible to translate directly not only into Chinese but also into English. According to the original meaning, the proper rendering for *the Holy Spirit* here should be *the Spirit the Holy*. You were sealed with the Spirit the Holy, who is also the pledge of our inheritance.

> And do not grieve the Holy Spirit of God, in whom you were sealed unto the day of redemption. (4:30)

The two passages above give us the overall subject matter: how the Holy Spirit of God is in us as the seal and the pledge. When you believed in Christ, you were sealed with the Holy Spirit. As long as you truly believe in Christ, this Spirit will surely be impressed as a seal in you. Today in Christianity there is a wrong teaching that is intimidating. Whenever certain ones meet a person, they ask, "Have you received the Holy Spirit?" After being asked such a question, many become confused and are not clear whether they have received the Holy Spirit. However, Ephesians 1:13-14 says that since you have believed, you have received. As long as you have believed, surely you have received. You have received the Holy Spirit as the seal; you have been sealed to show that you are God's inheritance. The Holy Spirit is also the pledge, guaranteeing that God belongs to you. The seal attests that we belong to God, whereas the pledge guarantees that God belongs to us. From the day we believed in the Lord, God has put His Spirit in us, impressed His Spirit in us, as a seal, attesting that we are God's, and as a pledge, guaranteeing that God is ours. From then on, we have become God's inheritance and God has become our portion. For us to be God's inheritance requires the seal of God upon us; for God to be our portion requires a pledge. In Greek the word for *pledge* has numerous meanings. It means "guarantee," "sample," or "foretaste." The Holy Spirit is put in us as our foretaste of God. The Holy Spirit being so sweet in us tells us that God is so sweet to us. This is a sample, a foretaste, and a guarantee, guaranteeing that God belongs to us.

In Ephesians only these two portions mention "the Spirit the Holy." Other places also mention the spirit, but often as "spirit," referring to the mingled spirit as the mingling of the Spirit of God with our spirit, as mentioned in 1 Corinthians 6:17: "He who is joined to the Lord is one spirit." In this one spirit there is the Spirit of God and there is also our spirit.

This may be compared to tea water. The tea is in the water, and the water is in the tea. If you say it is tea, that is correct; if you say it is water, that is also correct. But to describe it in a more detailed way, you may say it is "tea-water"; actually the two are mingled as one. The Spirit of God may be likened to tea and our spirit may be likened to water. When the Spirit of God is mingled with our spirit, the two spirits then become one spirit. This is the spirit referred to in Romans 8 and in Ephesians numerous times.

Ephesians shows us that this sealing and pledging Spirit is doing a work in us which consists of eight points: first, revealing; second, uniting; third, building; fourth, strengthening; fifth, renewing; sixth, filling; seventh, fighting; and eighth, praying. These are covered in the six chapters of Ephesians.

THE REVEALING SPIRIT

That the God of our Lord Jesus Christ, the Father of glory, may give to you a spirit of wisdom and revelation in the full knowledge of Him. (1:17)

This revealing Spirit is the Spirit who is joined with our spirit as one spirit. It is in this spirit that we know the Lord.

This Spirit enables us to see and comprehend the plan which God has formulated in eternity, the spiritual blessings in the heavenlies which He has given to us, the power which He has manifested in Christ, the hope of His calling to the saints, the riches of the glory of His inheritance in the saints, and the surpassing greatness of His power toward the believers. All these spiritual matters require the Spirit's revelation.

The mystery of Christ, which in other generations was not made known to the sons of men, as it has now been revealed to His holy apostles and prophets in spirit. (3:4b-5)

God's revelation to us today is in the Spirit. The first function of this Spirit in us is to reveal. He reveals the mystery of God, the acts of God, the riches of Christ, and the spiritual things. Many times we listen to messages, read spiritual books, and study the Bible by our mind, so there is no revelation. If you would close your eyes, call back your mind, return to your spirit, and linger a little while in your spirit, you will be enlightened within, and you will be able to see and have revelation. This is the function of revealing manifested by this Spirit. Many times you reason, debate, and discuss concerning the mystery of God and the matter of the church, yet the more you discuss, the more confused you are, and the more you cannot agree with one another. This is because you are in your mind. If you would abandon your mind, your reasoning, reject your emotion, and turn your whole being back to your spirit and remain in your spirit for a while, everything will be clear. Sometimes you need to pray, and once you pray you become clear. For this reason, many times we should pray instead of debate. When we pray, we get into the spirit, and in the spirit we are illuminated.

THE UNITING SPIRIT

For through Him we both have access in one Spirit unto the Father. (2:18)

We both have access unto the Father not by being inspired by the Spirit but by being in one Spirit. The Jews and the Gentiles could not be one; there was a solid wall between them. However, the Spirit is in the Jewish brothers, and the same Spirit is also in the Gentile brothers. Thus, in one Spirit they have become one. Hence, this Spirit is the uniting Spirit.

Being diligent to keep the oneness of the Spirit in the uniting bond of peace. (4:3)

This oneness is in the Spirit, and this Spirit is the oneness. The work He is doing in us is a revealing work and a uniting work. The more we debate about doctrine, the more we are separated; the more we debate, the greater the distance between us. However, if we would turn to our spirit, the result will be oneness. The fluorescent lamps in a room are separated outwardly, but they are joined in the electrical current to become one entity. Likewise, in ourselves you are you, and I am I; however, in the Spirit we are one.

THE BUILDING SPIRIT

In whom you also are being built together into a dwelling place of God in spirit. (2:22)

God's dwelling place, God's building, is built by the Spirit in our spirit. When we live in this Spirit, we have revelation; when we live in this Spirit, we keep the oneness; and when we live in this Spirit, we are built together.

One Body and one Spirit. (4:4a)

The Spirit is in the Body; hence, there is one Body and there is one Spirit. If we do not live in the Spirit, building becomes a mere doctrine, and so does coordination. Both the building and the coordination are in the Spirit. It is for this reason that we need to learn to live in the Spirit.

THE STRENGTHENING SPIRIT

That He would grant you, according to the riches of His glory, to be strengthened with power through His Spirit into the inner man. (3:16)

The inner man is our new man, our regenerated spirit, whereas the outer man is our soul. Our self is our soul; the Lord is in our spirit. Our soul is the outer man; our spirit is the inner man. Many saved ones are very strong in their soul but very weak in their spirit. In other words, their outer man is strong, but their inner man is weak. Hence, they do not have much experience of the Lord. For this reason the apostle Paul prayed that God would strengthen our spirit with His Spirit to make our spirit strong. Hence, the Spirit who is in us is the strengthening Spirit.

THE RENEWING SPIRIT

And that you be renewed in the spirit of your mind. (4:23)

At this stage the Spirit is no longer only in our spirit but has spread into our mind to become the spirit of the mind. For building we need transformation, and for transformation we need renewing. Romans 12 also refers to our being transformed by the renewing of the mind. How do we have this transformation by renewing? It is by having the Spirit in our mind. Unless the Spirit spreads to our mind, we cannot be renewed. Therefore, the Spirit must spread. If we frustrate the Spirit, there is no possibility for us to be transformed. God must spread to our mind so that our mind can become the spirit of the mind. It is in the spirit of the mind that we are renewed.

THE FILLING SPIRIT

And do not be drunk with wine…but be filled in spirit. (5:18)

When the spirit occupies the mind, the will, and the emotion, this means that the mind, the will, and the emotion are filled with the spirit. Thus, the spirit rules over the entire being and occupies the entire being. The word s*pirit* here does not have a definite article; it denotes neither the Holy Spirit nor our spirit in a definite way. Rather, it refers to the spirit formed out of two spirits. We have this spirit in us, but it is still not in our mind, emotion, or will. This spirit is only in our spirit; it has yet to enter into every part of our being. Now we need to let this spirit spread into every part of our being so that our entire being is filled with the spirit. Many people today talk about being filled with the Holy Spirit. Actually they are referring merely to the outpouring of the Holy Spirit. To have the outpouring is an outward matter, whereas to be filled is an inward matter.

When we repented and were saved, the Lord came into us. At that time our mind was turned, our emotion loved the Lord, and our will decided to receive Him. We opened our heart to the Lord, and He came in with rejoicing. However, gradually our mind, our emotion, and our will become closed to the Lord, and we shut Him up in our spirit. Some do it sooner, while others do it later. Eventually, your spirit becomes a prison. The Lord Jesus has found a prison instead of a dwelling place after He came into us. Do you know the difference between a prison and a dwelling place? You can go in and out freely in a dwelling place but not in a prison. Brothers and sisters, is the Lord Jesus residing in you or being imprisoned in you? Do you give the Lord Jesus freedom? Do not lock Him up any longer. Rather, open your heart again; turn your mind, emotion, and will to Him again. Then He is able to spread outward, and the result of this spreading is that He makes His home in your heart. Then He occupies your entire being, and every part of your being is filled with Him.

It would be a wonderful thing if some of us Christians could be occupied by the Lord within five years. The common situation is that we are constantly struggling with the Lord. In the morning we give our whole being to the Lord, but in the evening we take back one half. Then the next morning we take back another quarter, and in the end only a quarter is left. The Lord is frustrated within you, but all He can do is to wait patiently. After two weeks He comes to draw you again. Therefore, you repent and confess your sins again. Your mind is turned to Him and your emotion wants Him. You do this in the morning, yet at noon you change your mind again. Therefore, the Lord has been struggling with us for many years.

However, brothers and sisters, the Lord will always win. You can never win. If He cannot subdue you in one year, He will wait for five years. If He cannot subdue you in five years, He will wait for ten years. If He cannot subdue you in this age, in the coming age He will subdue you. But if you let Him get through sooner, you will be happy and He will also be happy. Otherwise, He will suffer and you also will suffer.

THE FIGHTING SPIRIT

And receive...the sword of the Spirit, which spirit is the word of God. (6:17)

The sword of the Spirit is obviously for fighting. Therefore, this Spirit is also the fighting Spirit. When you are occupied by and filled with the Spirit, you are equipped to fight the spiritual battle for the Lord.

THE PRAYING SPIRIT

Praying at every time in spirit. (v. 18)

This spirit does not refer to the Holy Spirit but to the spirit formed out of two spirits. We need to pray in this spirit.

Dear brothers and sisters, these eight items are the work of the Spirit of life in us as the seal and pledge. Through these eight items of work, He coordinates us into the Body and builds us into the church. When you turn to your spirit, you have the light and revelation concerning the church, the revelation concerning the mystery of Christ. You are also one with others. Since you are one, you are built and your spirit is strengthened. When you are strengthened, you are renewed; when you are renewed, you are filled; when you are filled, you are equipped to fight. It is in the fighting spirit that you pray. You pray for the spread of God's kingdom and for the revelation of the mystery of God. This is the church life and the Body life. The Body life is in this Spirit. This is the Spirit in Ephesians.

CHAPTER SEVEN

PHILIPPIANS AND COLOSSIANS

> For I know that for me this will turn out to salvation through your petition and the bountiful supply of the Spirit of Jesus Christ, according to my earnest expectation and hope that in nothing I will be put to shame, but with all boldness, as always, even now Christ will be magnified in my body, whether through life or through death. For to me, to live is Christ. (Phil. 1:19-21a)

In this portion of the Word, the fact that Christ will be magnified as always whether through life or through death is mentioned together with the bountiful supply of the Spirit of Jesus Christ. This proves that the supply of the Spirit is absolutely related to the magnification of Christ.

> Not that I speak according to lack, for I have learned, in whatever circumstances I am, to be content. I know also how to be abased, and I know how to abound; in everything and in all things I have learned the secret both to be filled and to hunger, both to abound and to lack. I am able to do all things in Him who empowers me. (4:11-13)

The apostle was content in whatever circumstances he was because he had learned the secret of doing all things "by depending on" Christ who strengthened him (Chinese Union Version). According to the Greek, *by depending on* should be rendered *in*. The apostle was able to do all things in the One who empowered him. There is a great difference between these two translations. For example, when we ride on a boat, strictly speaking, we are in the boat. When we board a boat, we get into the boat and sail by staying in the boat. We can walk, eat, sleep, play, and work in the boat without affecting its ability to sail on. This is what it means to be in the boat. In contrast, to depend on or hang on to the boat, I have to use my strength. It is dependable if I have the strength. However, if I let go because I have no more strength, then it is no longer dependable. Please remember that our dependence on the Lord is not outward but inward. Since you are in Him, whether or not you depend on Him, you are already in Him. As long as you are in Him, you have rest. This was Paul's secret.

> Only, conduct yourselves in a manner worthy of the gospel of Christ, that whether coming and seeing you or being absent, I may hear of the things concerning you, that you stand firm in one spirit, with one soul striving together along with the faith of the gospel. (1:27)

> If there is therefore any encouragement in Christ, if any consolation of love, if any fellowship of spirit, if any tender-heartedness and compassions. (2:1)

> For we are the circumcision, the ones who serve by the Spirit of God and boast in Christ Jesus and have no confidence in the flesh. (3:3)

PHILIPPIANS—THE EXPERIENCING SPIRIT

The book of Philippians has a special position in the Bible, which is to show us how to experience Christ. Philippians is a book on the experience of Christ. We need to see that these three small books, Galatians, Ephesians, and Philippians, are connected. After them, there is the book of Colossians. Hence, there is a total of four short books. The fact that these four books were put together is very meaningful, and I believe that their sequence is the arrangement of the Holy Spirit. Galatians tells us that Christ is our life, Christ is revealed in us, Christ lives in us, and Christ is being formed in us. We need to live in Christ, who is everything to us. After Galatians, there is Ephesians. If we truly live by Christ and take Christ as our life, the church immediately emerges. Christ as life produces the church. Hence, Galatians is on Christ as life, whereas Ephesians is on the church as the Body of Christ.

At this point it seems that everything is complete, so why do we still need Philippians? Please remember that Galatians merely speaks about Christ as life, but it does not show us how to experience Christ. Hence, after Ephesians, there is another book, Philippians, which shows us how to experience Christ. Philippians has four chapters. Chapter one shows us Christ as our manifestation; chapter two, Christ as our pattern; chapter three, Christ as our goal; and chapter four, Christ as our power. You may write in your Bible: manifestation, pattern, goal, and power or strength.

After Philippians, the book of Colossians shows us that the One who is the Head is everything. He is God's centrality and universality, He has the preeminence in all things, and He is all and in all. This reaches the pinnacle. Therefore, when you view these four books together, they are very meaningful.

MANIFESTING CHRIST IN OUR ENVIRONMENT THROUGH THE BOUNTIFUL SUPPLY OF THE SPIRIT OF JESUS CHRIST

Philippians gives us four aspects concerning the experience of Christ. The first aspect is in our environment, in our circumstances. The apostle said that whether through life or through death he was bold, as always, to have Christ magnified in his body. He also said that he had learned, in whatever circumstances he was, to be content and that he could do all things in Christ. This shows that the apostle experienced Christ in any kind of environment. How? He said that it was through the bountiful supply of the Spirit of Jesus Christ.

Thank God that in the New Testament there is the phrase *the Spirit of Jesus Christ*. The Spirit of Jesus is related to the Lord's incarnation. After His death and resurrection, we have the Spirit of Jesus Christ. This Spirit has many elements, including the Father, the Son, the Spirit, humanity, human living, the effectiveness of death, and the power of resurrection. Hence, the bountiful supply of such a Spirit is all-inclusive.

The Greek word for *bountiful supply* is a particular term as an allusion. In ancient Greece, the *choragus*, the leader of a stage chorus or dance, was responsible for the needs of all the members of the chorus in their living and in their performances. The choragus was responsible to supply whatever they needed. When the apostle Paul wrote the book of

Philippians, he used this particular term to describe how bountiful and rich the supply of the Spirit of Jesus Christ is, which is truly an all-inclusive, bountiful supply. Hence, in any circumstance His supply is sufficient for us. Whether in life or in death, whether in poverty or in wealth, whether in abasement or in exaltation, in whatever circumstance, He supplies. In Him is the all-inclusive, bountiful supply that enables us to meet any kind of environment and thus experience Christ, live Christ, and manifest Christ.

Dear brothers and sisters, I believe we all know this doctrine, so now let us apply it. For example, your husband may persecute you and give you a difficult time at home. The more you think about the situation, the more difficult it is. The more you try to deal with the situation, the more helpless you become. The more you try to reason with your husband, the more reasons he has. None of these ways work. What then is the proper way? It is very simple. When you are having a hard time, when you are being oppressed, you should turn back to your spirit. In your spirit is the Spirit of the Lord Jesus, the all-inclusive Spirit as the all-effective dose. Forget about your husband; do not care about being persecuted, nor try to reason with him, nor look for an outward remedy. Simply turn back to your spirit to contact the Spirit. This Spirit who is in you gives you comfort, sympathy, support, and strength to offset all kinds of oppression. This Spirit also has the transcending power that enables you to mount up with wings. Then you can praise, you can soar, you can sing hallelujah, and you feel that you are on the throne. After such a contact, your husband's persecution may still be there, but you do not sense the hardship because you are transcendent. The Spirit of Jesus Christ sustains you within to go through the suffering. He is the Spirit who suffered persecution and the Spirit who passed through death and entered into resurrection. The moment you contact Him, you are strengthened within.

PREACHING THE GOSPEL TO SINNERS
BY EXERCISING THE SPIRIT

The second aspect is to manifest Christ to sinners in preaching the gospel. This is to be in one spirit, with one soul striving together for the advancement of the gospel, as referred to in 1:27. If we want to manifest Christ, we must not forget the preaching of the gospel, and we must preach by exercising the spirit. For Christ to be magnified in any circumstance we need to preach the gospel to sinners by exercising our spirit. Without preaching the gospel, we will be short of one aspect in our experience of Christ.

From now on we should actively advance the gospel on the whole island of Taiwan. We have been here for over a decade, and we have received enough edification and nurturing from the Lord. We also have a good foundation in the administration and building of the church. Now we should stir up the whole church to go out and strive together for the preaching of the gospel.

We should give messages to prepare the hearts of the brothers and sisters. We need to teach them how to invite guests and pray for the gospel. We also need to instruct them how to make a list of the names of their relatives, friends, neighbors, colleagues, and any other acquaintances. They should see how many of those on the list are saved ones and how many are unsaved ones, and then learn to pick up the burden to invite the unsaved ones and preach the gospel to them. Furthermore, we need to train the brothers and sisters how to have gospel visitations and bring the ones who have believed to be baptized in the church. If we would actively promote this, I believe that within two years the number of the brothers and sisters on the whole island of Taiwan will increase at least onefold.

You should not have the notion that since you pursue Christ and know Christ, you can neglect the preaching of the gospel. No! By reading the book of Philippians you can see that even though it stresses our experience and manifestation of Christ, it especially brings up the matter of gospel preaching. Philippians 1 says, "He who has begun in you a good work will complete it until the day of Christ Jesus" (v. 6). What is the good work? The good work is to strive together to preach the gospel with one soul. Do we want to manifest Christ? We cannot manifest Christ by closing our door or by taking care of our own interests in seclusion. We need to manifest Christ in front of thousands of sinners, and we need to release Christ, minister Christ, and preach Christ from our spirit to the sinners. This is the genuine manifestation of Christ.

In 1949 when we were in Shanghai, almost all the brothers and sisters had some gospel tracts with them wherever they went. It seems this practice is rare today. Some people who may be either truly spiritual or falsely spiritual say that these activities are human works. If these are human works, then may I ask you: What are divine works? Where are the works which they called "divine works"? Oh, we need to smash these concepts! How can we manifest Christ unless we preach the gospel to hundreds and thousands of sinners? As the Body of Christ, the church must take care of all aspects. We should have the zeal for the gospel. Today some have been speaking in tongues for months, yet they have not been able to save even one person, so what is the use of their speaking in tongues? We may be inarticulate in presenting the truths, but we can fellowship with the Lord in spirit, we can love Him, and we can also love the souls of sinners. If we earnestly preach our Lord from our spirit to the sinners, then we are those who truly know Christ and truly manifest Christ. I beg you to rise up and preach the gospel from now on.

Our preaching of the gospel is also a matter in the spirit. You must contact the spirit if you want to preach the gospel. Otherwise, you will not be able to lead people to salvation. If you present the truths to others according to your mind, you may be able to make them understand, but you cannot make them alive or cause them to be regenerated. To help others to be regenerated, your spirit must be living. Some brothers are very smart and intelligent, so when they preach the gospel, they use their reasoning. Instead of exercising and contacting the spirit, they argue with others by reasoning. After a great deal of argument, they are able to defeat their listeners. However, being defeated does not equal being saved. I have seen many who were defeated but remained unsaved. However, I have also seen another kind of story. There are two or three brothers who are simple-minded, and even though they are not good with words, they are burning in spirit. When they lead others to believe in the Lord, they do not care about preaching the truths logically. Instead, they simply help people to pray. After a time of prayer, even a person with a hardened heart can touch the spirit and be saved. Therefore, preaching the gospel is not a matter of exercising our intellect but a matter of exercising our spirit to touch others' spirit.

Dear brothers and sisters, the power of the gospel lies not with the good presentation of the truth but with the release of the spirit. You must use your spirit to touch others' spirit. If you are bustling in your mind but cold in your spirit, even though you are able to present the truth clearly, no one will be saved. In preaching the gospel, first, we must have "thick skin"; second, we must have a simple mind; and third, we must have a burning spirit. Even if you scold me and hate me, I will still preach the gospel. If you show great zeal toward others, once they touch the spirit, they will be saved. Only in this way can you manifest Christ in the preaching of the gospel.

FELLOWSHIPPING WITH THE SAINTS IN SPIRIT

The third aspect is to have fellowship with the saints in spirit. We are members one of another, and we are brothers and sisters one to another. This is not a matter of friendship, nor a matter of a meeting of the minds, nor a matter of being fellow countrymen or fellow alumni. These relationships are of the flesh. Our fellowship is not in these relationships but in spirit.

Dear brothers and sisters, are the spirits of all the brothers and sisters opened? Is there fellowship among them? Can your spirit flow out to others? Can others' spirit flow into you? If we say we manifest Christ and experience Christ, we cannot be silent to sinners, refraining from preaching the gospel to them, nor can we isolate ourselves from the saints, being closed to them in spirit. Our fellowshipping spirit should be opened toward all the saints. Instead of demanding, criticizing, and condemning others, we minister to them, receive them, love them, and have fellowship with them, including even the most immature ones. I do not make distinctions between those who are exalted and those who are lowly or between those who are spiritual and those who are not. As long as someone is a brother, I simply love him, and whatever supply or fellowship he affords me, I simply receive. We should not set up a spiritual standard and have fellowship only with those who can come up to that standard. Our spirit must be opened to have fellowship with all the saints without discrimination. We should open our spirit to enjoy others and let others open their spirit to enjoy us. We should never try to do a particular work or set up a small circle within the church. Instead, we should be impartial toward all.

Dear brothers and sisters, history tells us that those who maintain a special fellowship eventually become "childless old people." You do not see them leading others to salvation, nor do you see them helping others to love the Lord. This is barrenness and abnormal development. This kills the Body. We must open our spirit to supply others and to receive supply from them as well. We can manifest Christ only by having fellowship without partiality.

WORSHIPPING GOD IN SPIRIT

The fourth aspect is to worship God in spirit. The first aspect covered in Philippians is that the Spirit is for our situations, another aspect is that the Spirit is for the gospel, still another aspect is that the Spirit is for fellowship, and the final aspect is that the Spirit is for worship. We have these four aspects: toward the environment, toward sinners, toward the saints, and toward God.

We worship God by the Spirit of God. Before he was saved, Paul had many merits according to his flesh, but he said that now he served God, worshipped God, in the Spirit and not in the flesh. This tells us that whenever we come to worship God, to serve God, we must reject our natural being, our self, our soul, and our flesh. We must only be in the Spirit. Hence, the secret to being a Christian is to exercise the spirit and live in the spirit. We must learn this secret if we want to manifest Christ.

After speaking about these four aspects of the experience and manifestation of Christ, the book of Philippians gives us a conclusion in 4:23: "The grace of the Lord Jesus Christ be with your spirit." Grace is the Lord Himself. This is similar to what 2 Timothy 4:22 says: "The Lord be with your spirit." We need to worship God in spirit and enjoy Him as grace.

COLOSSIANS

Colossians is a book on Christ being the Head of the church and having the first place in all things.

> Who also has made known to us your love in the Spirit. Therefore we also, since the day we heard of it, do not cease praying and asking on your behalf that you may be filled with the full knowledge of His will in all spiritual wisdom and understanding. (1:8-9)

Our love is in the Spirit and our understanding is of the Spirit. Our understanding is for us to understand God's will, which is concerning Christ, the church, and the mystery of God. Love is for us to live out what we comprehend in our understanding, and it is for others. This requires us to be in the Spirit. We need spiritual understanding to know and comprehend Christ, and this understanding should be in the Spirit. What we express as love should also be in the Spirit. This is the Spirit in Colossians.

Chapter Eight

FIRST AND SECOND THESSALONIANS—
THE SPIRIT OF SANCTIFICATION

> For our gospel did not come to you in word only, but also in power and in the Holy Spirit. (1 Thes. 1:5)

> And you...having received the word in much affliction with joy of the Holy Spirit. (v. 6)

In the term *the Holy Spirit* mentioned in the two verses quoted above, the word *Holy* is an emphasized word. These two verses say that the preaching of the gospel is in the Holy Spirit and that the receiving of the word, the receiving of the gospel, is also in the Holy Spirit. The Thessalonians received the gospel with joy of the Holy Spirit. The history of a Christian begins with the receiving of the gospel in the Holy Spirit.

> Consequently, he who rejects, rejects not man but God, who also gives His Holy Spirit to you. (4:8)

The Holy Spirit mentioned in this verse is a term with very strong emphasis in Greek. A better rendering of this term is *the Spirit the Holy.*

> Do not quench the Spirit. (5:19)

The Spirit here refers to the Spirit of the Lord who is in us and who is joined with our spirit as one spirit.

> But we ought to thank God always concerning you, brothers beloved of the Lord, because God chose you from the beginning unto salvation in sanctification of the Spirit and belief of the truth. (2 Thes. 2:13)

These are the only places in 1 and 2 Thessalonians that mention the Spirit, but they all are very meaningful. In these verses the apostle was saying to the Thessalonians, "The gospel was preached to you in the Holy Spirit, and you received the gospel in the joy of the Holy Spirit. After you received the gospel in this way, God has given to you 'the Spirit the Holy,' that is, His Holy Spirit. You should not quench this Holy Spirit who has entered into you and has mingled with your spirit to be one spirit—two spirits having become one spirit. And what kind of work is this Spirit doing in you? He is doing the work of sanctification to sanctify you over and over again."

> And the God of peace Himself sanctify you wholly, and may your spirit and soul and body be preserved complete, without blame, at the coming of our Lord Jesus Christ. Faithful is He who calls you, who also will do it. (1 Thes 5:23-24)

> So that He may establish your hearts blameless in holiness before our God and Father at the coming of our Lord Jesus with all His saints. (3:13)

CONCERNING SOME TITLES OF THE HOLY SPIRIT

For the sake of some brothers and sisters who are not clear concerning certain titles, such as the Spirit of God and the Holy Spirit, let us have a brief review. In the Old Testament, especially in the books of Isaiah and Jeremiah, the Spirit of God is always called the Spirit of Jehovah. Jehovah is God, and the Spirit of Jehovah is the Spirit of God. In the Chinese Union Version, there are two or three places in the Old Testament which use the title *the Holy Spirit,* but that is an inaccuracy in translation. Strictly speaking, such a title is not used in the Old Testament. This title did not exist until Mary became pregnant and was about to give birth to the Lord Jesus. It was not formally used until the mention in Luke 1 and Matthew 1 concerning the Lord Jesus' incarnation and His being conceived in a virgin.

The title *the Holy Spirit* means that the Spirit of God is "the Holy"; He is *the Spirit the Holy* of God. In the universe only God Himself is holy, and only God Himself is holiness itself. Everything else, all of creation, is not holy. Now God was to be incarnated through this Spirit that He might make the unholy created men holy and bring them into holiness. You must not have the concept that being unholy is bad or evil. Actually, being unholy does not mean being evil; rather, it means being void of God's nature. This is similar to saying that just because a certain object is not gold does not mean that it is dirty or useless. In man's religious mind there is an incorrect concept; whenever we hear that something is not holy, we automatically think it refers to defilement. This concept needs to be corrected. Holiness is God Himself; it is the nature of God. As we have said before, love is God's heart, righteousness is God's way of doing things, God's procedure, and holiness is God's nature, God's substance. Therefore, being unholy means being void of God's nature or essence. You may remember that in the Old Testament, the boards in the tabernacle were made of acacia wood overlaid with gold. Wood equals humanity, and gold equals divinity. Originally, we had only humanity but no divinity; we were like wood without gold. This does not mean that the wood is decayed or defiled. This is also what we mean when we refer to being unholy.

When man was created, nothing in the universe had the nature of God. Only God Himself had the divine nature. None of the millions of creatures were holy; only God Himself was holy. But one day this God, who is Spirit and who is holy, became flesh to be mingled with man and to put on humanity. He did this because He wanted to make man holy, to sanctify man. The basic principle of incarnation is that "the Spirit the Holy" of God entered into the unholy man to make him holy. In other words, He wanted to make the man who was without God's nature into a man with God's nature. Thus, from this time onward, the title *the Holy Spirit* appeared in the Bible. Strictly speaking, therefore, the Holy Spirit is for the purpose of making the unholy man holy, that is, making the man who is without God's nature into a man with God's nature.

I think the brothers and sisters are clear about my speaking. You may say that God in eternity was Jehovah, and you may also say that He was God. At that time, the Spirit of God was called the Spirit of God and the Spirit of Jehovah as well. It was not until later, when God became flesh, that the Spirit of God began to be called the Holy Spirit. After the incarnated God entered into death and also into resurrection, His Spirit had a new title, that is, the life-giving Spirit. It was at this time that the incarnated God became the life-giving Spirit, because He had passed through death and resurrection. His death solved all the problems between man and God, and His resurrection released the life that was within Him. Therefore, by this time He was not merely the Spirit, but He was also the Spirit who gives life.

The Spirit was first the Spirit of God because He was God. God is Spirit, and the Spirit is the Spirit of God. Later, at the time of God's incarnation He became the Holy Spirit, that is, "the Spirit the Holy." He comes to make unholy man into holy man, that is, to make the man who is without the divine nature into a man with the divine nature. Therefore, He is the Holy Spirit. Then the Lord entered into death and resurrected. In this death and resurrection, the Spirit became the life-giving Spirit. Whose Spirit is this life-giving Spirit? He is "the Spirit of Jesus Christ." This Spirit can sometimes also be called "the Spirit of Jesus," and sometimes "the Spirit of Christ." Under what circumstances is He called "the Spirit of Jesus?" If you read Acts 16, you will see that *the Spirit of Jesus* is a title used in times of the apostles' sufferings for the Lord in hardships, in persecutions, in taking the way of poverty, and in being reproached for His sake. This is the Spirit who led Jesus of Nazareth to live a life of poverty on earth and to suffer persecution and shame. Therefore, Acts 16:7 refers to "the Spirit of Jesus." What about the Spirit of Christ? "The Spirit of Christ" is in Romans 8:9. Moreover, Romans 8:11 says that "if the Spirit of the One who raised Jesus from the dead dwells in you," then this One "will also give life to your mortal bodies." Therefore, Romans 8 does not emphasize the aspect of following the lowly Nazarene by suffering hardship, being put to shame, and taking the way of the cross. Rather, it emphasizes living out the Lord's life. Thus, the Spirit of Christ is mainly for resurrection. Romans 8 is a story of resurrection in which not only the spirit is made alive, but even the mortal body is also made alive. Hence, "the Spirit of Jesus" is one story and "the Spirit of Christ" is another story.

Moreover, Philippians 1 mentions "the Spirit of Jesus Christ," joining "Jesus" and "Christ" together. This is because in Philippians there is a story of suffering. The apostle seemed to be saying, "The bountiful supply of the Spirit of Jesus Christ will be my salvation. Even though I am here in prison, in bonds and chains, yet this Spirit, who is not only the Spirit of Jesus but also the Spirit of Christ, and not only the Spirit of suffering but also the Spirit of resurrection, will enable me to overcome the afflictions and bonds." Therefore, in Philippians, there is suffering and there is also release because the Spirit is the Spirit of Jesus Christ.

This Spirit of Jesus Christ is the life-giving Spirit. "The life-giving Spirit" refers to the function of the Spirit, whereas "the Spirit of Jesus Christ" is the title of the Spirit. Today this Spirit belongs to Jesus, to Christ, and to Jesus Christ. This Spirit, who is Christ Himself, gives us life. Therefore, there are not several spirits, but there is only one Spirit in several stages. Before the Word became flesh, the Spirit of God was simply the Spirit of God. But after the Word became flesh, the Spirit of God became the Holy Spirit, "the Spirit the Holy." Then later, after the Lord passed through death and resurrection, this Spirit became the life-giving Spirit, who belongs to Jesus Christ, so He is called the Spirit of Jesus, the Spirit of Christ, and the Spirit of Jesus Christ. We may use a handkerchief as an illustration. If you put a white handkerchief into a vat of blue dye, it becomes a blue handkerchief, and if you put the blue handkerchief into a vat of red dye, it becomes a purple handkerchief. The white handkerchief, the blue handkerchief, and the purple handkerchief are not three handkerchiefs; rather, they are one handkerchief in three stages.

FIRST AND SECOND THESSALONIANS—
THE SPIRIT OF SANCTIFICATION

Now let us come to 1 and 2 Thessalonians. The Spirit in 1 and 2 Thessalonians is the Spirit of sanctification. Brothers and sisters, I hope that you can see that the general subject of the New Testament Epistles is the life-giving Spirit. In Romans, this life-giving Spirit as the Spirit of sonship is conforming us to the image of God's Son. In 1 Corinthians, as the building Spirit He is building all of us together into one Body.

In 2 Corinthians, as the transforming Spirit He is transforming us, who were previously men of dust, into gold, silver, and precious stones for the building. In Galatians, as the Spirit for our living He enables us to live by Christ and live out Christ. In Philippians, He is the One who enables us to experience Christ in our practical living, to experience Christ in every situation and in every matter, and to experience Christ with respect to situations, sinners, saints, and God. In 1 and 2 Thessalonians, He is the Spirit of sanctification. He preaches the gospel to us and leads us to receive it, and then He comes into us as the Spirit of sanctification who constantly sanctifies us, preparing us to receive the coming Christ. We are in the process of sanctification, waiting for Him to sanctify us.

THE PROGRESSION OF GOD'S RECOVERY OF SANCTIFICATION

Holiness—Deliverance from Sin

The progression of God's recovery of the matter of sanctification is as follows: After the reformation with Luther, there was quite a long period of time in which the church did not pay attention to this matter. It was not until the eighteenth century that John Wesley and his companions began to stress the matter of holiness. At that time, however, they could be considered to have recovered only the term *holiness* but not the reality of holiness. Actually they recovered something erroneous. The holiness taught by John Wesley and his co-workers was one which required people to live a life of sinless perfection. Because of the influence of this teaching, some in Christianity have the concept that to be holy is to be sinless or to overcome sin; if one can overcome sin and be perfect, then one is considered holy.

Later, under this influence several groups emerged. For example, in the West there are various Wesleyan or Methodist churches which were produced from the teachings of John Wesley. They all teach the doctrine of holiness, which is to behave properly without mistakes, as taught by John Wesley. The word *Methodist,* derived from the English word *method,* denotes one whose behavior is proper, regulated, orderly, or one who behaves with decorum, observing all rules and regulations. This is the holiness they teach. From this, the Church of the Nazarene also emerged, and we may say that it strictly follows the teachings of John Wesley. Many people think that most of the Christian women in America curl their hair, wear make-up, and are very fashionable. In actuality, I can tell you that in the Church of the Nazarene in America the women are all very proper, and all avoid make-up and fashionable clothes. That is their holiness. Mrs. Cowman, who wrote the book *Streams in the Desert,* and her husband founded the Far East Missionary Society and worked mostly in Japan. They mainly did the work of helping people to be holy. Thus, the church established by the Far East Missionary Society in Japan is called the Holiness Church. This Holiness Church spread through Japan and came to Taiwan, where it was called the Holy Church. Both the Holy Church in Taiwan and the Holiness Church in Japan were brought in through the work of the Far East Missionary Society, which mainly preached the holiness as taught by John Wesley.

Positional Sanctification—Being Separated

After one century, in 1828, the British Brethren were raised up. The British Brethren represent a huge recovery in the matters of the truth and the study of the Scriptures. From the Scriptures they learned that the meaning of the word *holiness* does not emphasize purity but separation. They pointed out that the sanctification referred to in many passages in the Bible has no bearing on being without sin or without evil. Rather, it is mostly related to being separated. For example, in Matthew 23 the Lord Jesus said that the temple could sanctify the gold (v. 17). The gold had originally been kept in the shops or at home, so it was common and not holy, but when the gold was brought into the temple, the temple sanctified the gold. If holiness denotes being sinless, then does the gold in the shops have sins? By this we can see there is no thought of sin here. Thus, to be sanctified is to be separated; whatever is separated unto God is sanctified. The Lord Jesus also said that the altar sanctifies the bulls and sheep sacrificed upon it (v. 18). Originally a bull or a sheep was in its herd or in its flock and was common, not holy; however, now it has been separated out and offered up upon the altar. The altar separates and sanctifies it. Can the bull or the sheep have sins? They cannot. They are common but do not necessarily have sins. Furthermore, in 1 Timothy 4 Paul says that the food we eat is sanctified through intercession. Can milk and bread have sins? They cannot; however, when milk and bread are on the table, they are common if they have not passed through the Christians' prayers. After having passed through the Christians' prayers, the milk and bread are separated, sanctified.

Dispositional Sanctification— Adding the Element of God

Brothers and sisters, over thirty years ago when we spoke about sanctification, we taught the same doctrine that was taught by the Brethren. But as we studied the Bible again, we gradually learned that the word *sanctification* does not merely mean separation. Separation is on the negative side, but sanctification has also a positive meaning. In these recent years we have seen that we cannot truly say that sanctification does not include the meaning which John Wesley taught. What the Brethren taught is right also, but they overemphasized it. It is true that the gold is sinless, and the bull, the sheep, the bread, and the milk are also sinless, but today we cannot say that we do not have the problem of sin. There is no thought of sin in the separation of gold and in the separation of bulls, sheep, bread, and milk. However, you and I were sinful from the beginning, so we cannot say that when we are separated to become holy, there is no element of being delivered from sin. The matter of sanctification with respect to gold, bulls, sheep, milk, and bread does not have the significance of the deliverance from sin, but with respect to sinners such as you and I, God's separation includes our being separated from sin and being delivered from sin. If you have not been delivered from sin, how can you be separated unto God? Thus, this separation includes being delivered from sin, the world, the flesh, and all things and matters that are contrary to and against God.

Dear brothers and sisters, at the time of John Wesley, God's recovery of the truth of sanctification was only the recovery of the first step, that is, of purity. Later, at the time of the Brethren, it was the recovery of the second step, which was separation. And now, we see that it is not only separation. The Brethren spoke much, but it was only on the matter of being separated. They forgot the matter of being made holy. Sanctification is not only a matter of being delivered from sin or being separated unto God but also a matter of being made holy. How can we be made holy? It is by having God Himself added into us inwardly. When the element of God that is added into us increases, you and I become more separated from sin, from the world, and from the flesh. Moreover, the divine nature and image in us also increase. Therefore, sanctification is to put God and Christ into us and to release us from sin, the world, and the flesh. He does not only separate us, but He also makes us holy.

Transformation

Therefore, in its final step sanctification is simply transformation. In Christianity you can rarely hear a message on transformation. You can search through all the Christian bookstores, but you can hardly find one book on transformation. There are many books that speak about holiness and also many books that speak about separation, but it is difficult to find a book on transformation. This is because the light concerning this matter was not clear in the early days. Now this light has become more and more clear. Sanctification is not merely a matter of purity or separation but also a matter of being made holy.

What is it to be made holy? To be made holy is to have the element of God and of Christ added into us through the life-giving Spirit. In this way we are separated and made holy. Furthermore, once the element of God is added into us, there is transformation within us.

The sanctification taught by the Brethren is only separation, and it is really only positional separation and not dispositional separation. Today, however, the sanctification which we speak about is not only a positional change but also a dispositional change. When you take the gold out of the shops or homes and place it in the temple, this is merely a positional change. When you take bulls or sheep out of the herds or flocks and place them on the altar, or when you take bread from the bakery and place it onto a Christian's dinner plate, this too is merely a positional change. There has been no change of disposition. However, when 1 and 2 Thessalonians mention the Spirit of sanctification, this sanctification is not only a positional change but also a dispositional change. Today the life-giving Spirit in us is continually infusing and constituting Christ into us. Consequently, we do not have only a change of position, but we also have a change of disposition. Thus, we do not have mere separation, nor do we just have purity, but we also have holiness. The truth of sanctification includes these three matters: separation, purity, and holiness.

The ultimate result of sanctification is glorification. God has come into our spirit, then He is spreading outward into our soul to do the work of transformation, which is also the work of sanctification, and lastly He will transfigure our bodies. This is sanctification to the uttermost and is also glorification. Glorification is God expressed, God manifested. At that time, our condition from the inside to the outside will be God manifested.

THE SPIRIT OF HOLINESS
AND THE SANCTIFICATION OF THE SPIRIT

Now let us come back to 1 and 2 Thessalonians. These two books teach that the goal of the believers' living on earth is to await the Lord's coming. When we wait for the Lord's coming, our spirit, soul, and body are all sanctified. Who is doing this work of sanctification? It is the Spirit with our spirit mingled as one spirit who is doing this work. Thus, these two books show us that the apostle preached the gospel to us in the Holy Spirit, and we also received the gospel in the Holy Spirit, so God put "the Spirit the Holy," His Holy Spirit, into us to be mingled with our spirit as one spirit. Therefore, we should not quench this Spirit. Rather, we should allow this Spirit to do the work of sanctification daily in us. Because of the Spirit's sanctification we will eventually be completely saved, so that at His coming back our spirit and soul and body will be preserved complete, without blame (1 Thes. 5:23). This should be the way we await the Lord's coming. In the process of sanctification we are waiting for the Lord.

This sanctification is carried out by the Holy Spirit. However, there is a particular point to consider here. In Romans we have "the Spirit of holiness" (1:4), while here we have "sanctification of the Spirit" (2 Thes. 2:13). These two terms, *holiness* and *sanctification,* have the same Greek root with different endings. In Romans, in the phrase *the Spirit of holiness, holiness* refers to the nature of the Spirit. In 2 Thessalonians, in the phrase *sanctification of the Spirit,* the word *sanctification* refers to the effect of the Spirit. The Spirit of holiness is the Spirit with the holy nature, while sanctification of the Spirit refers to holiness as the result of the Spirit's working in us.

Thank and praise God that in the first book of the Epistles there is "the Spirit of holiness," but in 2 Thessalonians a result has been produced, that is, "sanctification of the Spirit." In the very beginning there was the Spirit of God, but now He is the Spirit of Jesus, the Spirit of Christ, the life-giving Spirit, and the Spirit of sonship doing the work of sanctification in us with God's holy nature. Thus, He is the Spirit with the holy nature who is doing the work of sanctification in us, and after we pass through the process of sanctification, He will produce the result of sanctification, which is the Spirit's sanctification. We thank God that eventually we will have not only the Spirit of holiness but also the Spirit's sanctification! At the beginning we only have the Spirit of holiness coming into us, but eventually we will be sanctified by this Spirit. We have the process of sanctification, and we also have the result of sanctification. This is the work that the Spirit is doing in us.

CHAPTER NINE

FIRST AND SECOND TIMOTHY, TITUS, AND PHILEMON

FIRST AND SECOND TIMOTHY— THE GUARDING SPIRIT

The Speaking Spirit

Let us first look at the book of 1 Timothy. First Timothy 4:1 says, "But the Spirit says expressly that in later times some will depart from the faith, giving heed to deceiving spirits and teachings of demons." I believe we all understand now that the mention of the Spirit in this way indicates that this Spirit is not purely the objective Holy Spirit, but the objective Holy Spirit becoming the subjective Holy Spirit dwelling in our spirit and being mingled with our spirit as one spirit. This Spirit was speaking in the apostle Paul and in the saints. This is not like the prophets prophesying in the Old Testament according to the Spirit of Jehovah who descended upon them outwardly. With us in the New Testament, it is the Spirit of life dwelling in our spirit and being mingled with us as one spirit speaking the word of God.

When the apostle wrote the Epistles to Timothy, the church was already in degradation and confusion. At such times, God does not care much for the outward prophesying of the prophets because it is merely the speaking of some extraordinary words by the prophets after the objective Spirit of God had come upon them. That was the Old Testament way of prophesying, but it is not considered important in the New Testament. I am not saying that there is no such prophesying or that such prophesying is wrong. I am simply saying that it is not considered important. The New Testament pays attention to the fact that the Spirit of life comes into our spirit to be mingled with our spirit as one spirit and that we speak according to the feeling in our spirit. First Corinthians 7 is the best example of this. Obviously it was Paul speaking there because he said clearly that he was giving his opinion without having a commandment from the Lord. However, he eventually said, "I think that I also have the Spirit of God" (v. 40).

When you read the books of Isaiah, Jeremiah, and Ezekiel, however, and when you read the prophecies spoken by the prophets in the Old Testament, you can see that they were not the prophets' own way of speaking but rather God's way of speaking. When the Spirit of Jehovah came to, or descended upon, Jeremiah, he began to speak, "I, Jehovah, say this and that." The Old Testament prophets all spoke in God's "tone." However, when you read the New Testament Epistles, such as Romans, 1 and 2 Corinthians, Galatians, Ephesians, Philippians, and Colossians, you will notice that none of them has God's "tone." Rather, they were all written in the writer's tone. Although they were the writer's words, they were considered God's words. This is because in the New Testament age everything is in the principle of incarnation, which is the principle of God mingled with man. In the Old Testament it was the Spirit of God falling upon man and using man as a vessel, just as the Spirit of God fell upon a donkey and used the donkey as a vessel to speak human language. That was the Old Testament principle. According to the Old Testament principle, there was no mingling of God and man. Rather, there was only God descending upon man and using man as a mouth, a vessel, a trumpet. But the New Testament principle is different. In the New Testament God enters into man and mingles with man to become one entity. Consequently, it was Paul speaking, it was Paul writing to the saints in Corinth, and it was Paul commanding and speaking. When Paul spoke, however, the Spirit who was mingled with Paul also spoke. Thus, the tone of speaking in the New Testament is man's tone.

I am pointing out this matter with a purpose. Today you can see that the tongues spoken in the Pentecostal movement all sound like God's own speaking. They are all spoken in the first person: "I will do this or I will do that." Moreover, they frequently prophesy by saying: "O My people, My day has drawn near. Be prepared!" If you listen carefully to their words or expressions, you will notice that they are words found either in Isaiah or in Jeremiah. Brothers and sisters, you have to know that this is against the New Testament principle.

Please read the book of Acts. Does it have a record of such a prophecy spoken by the apostles? There is no such record either in Acts or in the Epistles. Today in the degradation of the church, you will be deceived if you listen to these outward speakings. Thus, in the time of the degradation of the church, the apostle Paul wrote a letter with this phrase: "The Spirit says expressly." It is not the objective Holy Spirit speaking to us, as people suppose. Rather, it is the Spirit of life who dwells in us and who has been mingled with our spirit into one spirit speaking within us.

The Spirit of Power, Love, and Sobermindedness

Second Timothy 1:7 says, "For God has not given us a spirit of cowardice, but of power and of love and of sobermindedness." The spirit that God has given us is such a spirit. According to the Chinese translation, it seems that this spirit denotes our human spirit. In actuality, however, this is still referring to the two spirits mingled to be one spirit. Today within us we have a mingled spirit, a spirit which is of power, of love, and of sobermindedness. Sometimes you are powerful, yet without love; at other times you are very weak, yet full of love. It is very difficult to have both at the same time. Furthermore, once we love, we cannot think clearly. Many times love makes people foolish, but if they are clear, they cannot love. After we discuss a matter and consider the people, we simply cannot love them anymore. It is wonderful that the Lord's word shows us that God has given us a spirit not only of power but also of love and of sobermindedness. This is a marvelous thing.

In the time of the church's degradation, these three items are necessary. Your spirit must be strong or else there will be confusion. However, while you have a strong spirit, you must not be without love, and at the same time you must not be without sobermindedness while you are paying attention to love. Otherwise, the church will be a confused mess. During the time of confusion, your spirit must be strong, loving, and sober. The opposite of the word *sobermindedness* is *drunk*. To be drunk is to be confused and disorderly. On the contrary, to be sober is to be clear, orderly, and transparent. Dear brothers and sisters, this truly is our present need. We need this kind of a spirit, a spirit with power, love, and sobermindedness, a spirit which is sober in love and loving in power. Only this kind of spirit is adequate for dealing with a confused situation and can meet the need of a degraded condition. What God has given us is such a spirit.

The Guarding Spirit

Furthermore, 2 Timothy 1:14 says, "Guard the good deposit through the Holy Spirit who dwells in us." Here, Paul seemed to be saying, "Timothy, you have followed me for so many years and have had so many good and spiritual things entrusted or revealed to you, so you must carefully guard this good deposit through the Holy Spirit who dwells in us. The church is degraded, the age has changed, men's hearts are different now, and everything is not the way it was, but you must carefully guard the good things, the things which have been entrusted to you and deposited in you over the years, through the Holy Spirit who dwells in you." In the church's degradation we need such a guarding Spirit to guard the deposit in us today of the things which we received in the past.

The final point is in 4:22, which says, "The Lord be with your spirit." This statement is not found in any of the other Epistles. What Paul meant by this word was: "O Timothy, I have already spoken so many messages to you, and this is my dying command and parting word to you. Before I die, I want to give you this word: 'The Lord be with your spirit.' The Lord is the Spirit, the life-giving Spirit, and this Spirit is with you in your spirit."

Thus, the Spirit in 1 and 2 Timothy is the guarding Spirit.

How does He guard us? From your reading, you can see that He is the indwelling Spirit who dwells in your spirit to make your spirit strong, loving, and soberminded. He is also speaking from within your spirit, showing you the degraded condition of this age. As such a Spirit He dwells in your spirit to be the guarding Spirit.

TITUS—THE RENEWING SPIRIT

Now we come to the book of Titus. In Titus there is only one passage that mentions the Spirit. Verses 5b-7 of chapter three say, "He saved us, through the washing of regeneration and the renewing of the Holy Spirit, whom He poured out upon us richly through Jesus Christ our Savior, in order that having been justified by His grace, we might become heirs according to the hope of eternal life." The renewing work of the Holy Spirit within us is almost the same as His work of transformation. He is the renewing Spirit whom God poured out upon us richly through Jesus Christ our Savior. The result of this outpouring is that we have been justified by His grace to become heirs according to the hope of eternal life. Thus, the goal of the outpouring of this Spirit is that we may become heirs of God and sons of God.

What is the difference between heirs and sons? Heirs are eligible to receive the inheritance. If a king has eight sons, only the eldest is the designated heir to inherit the throne. The other seven sons are just sons, not heirs. Today we are not just sons; we are also heirs. We have inherited all that God has given to us and all that God possesses. The renewing Spirit does a renewing work within us to make us not only sons but also heirs.

Let me repeat: God saved us through the washing of regeneration and the renewing of the Holy Spirit, whom God poured out upon us richly through Jesus Christ our Savior in order that, on the one hand, we may be justified by His grace, and on the other hand, we may become heirs according to the hope of eternal life. Justification is the first aspect, while eternal life is the second aspect. In this way we may become heirs of God.

PHILEMON—THE SPIRIT OF PRESENCE

Verse 25 of Philemon says, "The grace of the Lord Jesus Christ be with your spirit." In order to experience, enjoy, and fully taste the grace of the Lord, we must know the Spirit, because the grace of the Lord is in our spirit. The apostle Paul, realizing that nothing else was more important, gave a final word, saying, "The grace of the Lord Jesus Christ be with your spirit." In the books of 1 and 2 Timothy is the guarding Spirit, in the book of Titus is the renewing Spirit, and in the book of Philemon, we may say, is the Spirit of presence.

CHAPTER TEN

HEBREWS—THE SPIRIT OF GRACE

THE SPEAKING SPIRIT

The Epistle to the Hebrews firstly shows us that the Holy Spirit is the speaking Spirit. Hebrews 3:7-8 says, "Therefore, even as the Holy Spirit says, 'Today if you hear His voice, do not harden your hearts as in the provocation, in the day of trial in the wilderness.'" *The Holy Spirit* here is a very emphatic term; according to Greek, it is *the Spirit the Holy.* Therefore, the word spoken by the Holy Spirit here in Hebrews is different from the word spoken by the Spirit in 1 Timothy 4:1. What the Spirit says there in 1 Timothy 4:1 is not a quotation from the Old Testament but the sensation given to us by the Spirit in our spirit, whereas here in Hebrews the Holy Spirit speaks by quoting the words in the Old Testament.

Hebrews 9:8 says, "The Holy Spirit [lit., the Spirit the Holy] thus making this clear, that the way of the Holy of Holies has not yet been manifested while the first tabernacle still has its standing." You see again that the Holy Spirit uses a figure of the Old Testament. Whatever is spoken by "the Spirit the Holy," whatever is purely the word spoken by God, is a quotation from the Old Testament. Hence, it is the objective Spirit speaking the Old Testament words objectively. However, the word in 1 Timothy 4:1 is a subjective word; it is the feeling given to us from within by the Spirit who is mingled with us as one spirit.

Hebrews 10:15-16 says, "And the Holy Spirit also testifies to us, for after having said, 'This is the covenant which I will covenant with them after those days, says the Lord.'" Again, this is a quotation from the Old Testament. This is the objective Holy Spirit, not the subjective Spirit, speaking an objective word. Thus, it is again a quotation from the Old Testament. In 1 Timothy 4:1, however, when the subjective Spirit speaks in us a subjective word, He does not quote from the Old Testament. Do you see the difference? Whenever the objective word is spoken, it is "the Spirit the Holy" who speaks to us. Whenever the subjective word is spoken, it is the Holy Spirit mingled with our spirit as one spirit—the subjective spirit—who speaks. That is a feeling that we have from deep within and not a word quoted or a figure taken from the Old Testament.

Unlike the other Epistles, the Epistle to the Hebrews does not tell us from the outset who the author is. Rather, it says that God spoke of old through the prophets and speaks now through His Son. Therefore, when it quotes from the Old Testament, it does not do so like the other Epistles by saying that it is a word spoken by Isaiah or by Jeremiah. Rather, it says that it is the Holy Spirit's speaking. This is an amazing thing. The Epistle to the Hebrews does not indicate plainly the person who speaks but rather tells us that it is God who speaks, or the Holy Spirit who speaks. Thus, the Spirit in Hebrews is the speaking Spirit.

THE SPIRIT OF GRACE

Those who have once been enlightened and have tasted of the heavenly gift and have become partakers of the Holy Spirit. (Heb. 6:4)

By how much do you think he will be thought worthy of worse punishment who has trampled underfoot the Son of God and has considered the blood of the covenant by which he was sanctified a common thing and has insulted the Spirit of grace? (10:29)

These two verses show us that the Spirit in Hebrews has become the blessing of which we partake. The speaking Spirit has become the Spirit of grace for our enjoyment.

THE ETERNAL SPIRIT

Christ, who through the eternal Spirit offered Himself without blemish to God. (9:14)

The Lord Jesus' offering Himself to God on the cross was through the eternal Spirit. Therefore, the Spirit in Hebrews is also the eternal Spirit. These are the three aspects of the Spirit in Hebrews: the speaking Spirit, the Spirit of grace (the Spirit of enjoyment), and the eternal Spirit. It is easy to understand the speaking Spirit, and it is also easy to understand the Spirit of grace, the Spirit of enjoyment, but it is not so easy to understand the eternal Spirit. Many of us consider eternity as something in the future. However, in the Bible, eternity includes the entire span of time. May I ask you, brothers and sisters, when did the Lord Jesus offer Himself to God? In other words, when was the Lord Jesus put on the cross as a sin offering? According to history, the Lord Jesus was crucified on Calvary's mountain almost two thousand years ago, and standing in front of Him were His disciples including Peter and John. Thus, it is true that the Lord Jesus died for those who were His contemporaries. But how could He die for people such as Abel, Job, and Abraham, who were there many years before Him? Furthermore, how could He die for people like us, who are here many years after Him and who were not yet born at His time? I do not know if you can solve this. Here we need to read Hebrews 9:14, which says that Christ offered Himself without blemish to God through the eternal Spirit. According to His flesh, He was crucified at a certain time. However, according to the eternal Spirit, His crucifixion encompasses the entire span of time. Thus, according to the sense of time, Job and Abraham were before the crucifixion and we are after the crucifixion, but according to the sense of eternity, there is no differentiation between before and after. Christ in the eternal Spirit offered Himself to become our sin offering. There is no time element with His death. In our perception and in the historical sense, there is the time element. In God's view, however, there is no time element because God is eternal. Therefore, Revelation 13:8 speaks of "the Lamb who was slain from the foundation of the world." He was slain not just two thousand years ago but from the foundation of the world. His being slain meets the need of all sinners. Although His being slain was accomplished in time, in God's view He was slain in eternity. Thus,

He became an eternal sin offering. If your view is according to the flesh, He is Jesus the Nazarene who died two thousand years ago. However, in the eternal Spirit He died in the realm of eternity. His one offering accomplished redemption eternally because He died not only in the flesh but also in the eternal Spirit.

Hence, if we want to understand spiritual things, we must not remain in our mind. Instead, we must be in spirit. Once we are living in our mind, we are in time, but when we turn to our spirit, we enter into eternity. It is then that we are able to comprehend the things that transcend time.

Chapters five, six, nine, and ten of Hebrews all speak of eternity. Hence, this is truly a book concerning eternity. However, this is not the eternity in the future but the eternity that includes all needs and encompasses all time. In this book which deals with eternity, the Spirit is not only the speaking Spirit and the Spirit for our enjoyment but also the eternal Spirit. You can understand the things of eternity only in the eternal Spirit. In other words, you can understand the things of God which are in the realm of eternity only in the eternal Spirit.

Brothers and sisters, I believe that you can sense what I am saying. If you learn to always get out of your mind and turn to your spirit, your spirit will be freed from the restriction of your little mind. Our mind cannot comprehend the eternal things. Once you fall into the mind, your understanding becomes bound, confined in every way, and is unable to comprehend. However, once you reject your mind and get into your spirit, you become like one who has soared into space; you are released. Your created mind is limited, but you have been saved, and you have the eternal Spirit in you. This Spirit has neither beginning nor ending. You cannot find the start or the finish. In this Spirit you are able to understand the eternal things.

DISCERNING THE SPIRIT FROM THE SOUL
AND ENTERING INTO THE HOLY OF HOLIES

Now we come to Hebrews 4:12, which says, "For the word of God is living and operative and sharper than any two-edged sword, and piercing even to the dividing of soul and spirit and of joints and marrow, and able to discern the thoughts and intentions of the heart." The Holy Spirit, as the speaking Spirit, the Spirit of grace, the Spirit for our enjoyment, and the unlimited, eternal Spirit, dwells in our spirit today. Therefore, we must learn to discern our spirit from our soul. If you do not know how to discern the spirit from the soul, you will have no way to enjoy the Spirit of grace or to enter into the eternal Spirit. You will also have no way to hear the word of God or to understand the Bible. Many people think that a smart mind is required for the understanding of the Bible. This is not necessarily true. To understand the Bible requires us to enter into our spirit. Only when you are in your spirit will you be able to hear the speaking of the Holy Spirit. Your spirit is where He as the Spirit is, so you must divide your spirit from your soul.

Dear brothers and sisters, among all the Epistles in the New Testament, only Hebrews tells us to enter into the Holy of Holies (10:19), which is our spirit. Furthermore, 4:16 says to come forward to the throne of grace, which is the cover of the ark, which was within the Holy of Holies, in the Old Testament time.

We know that both with the ark and with the temple, there are three sections: the outer court, the Holy Place, and the Holy of Holies. In the outer court are the altar and the laver. The altar signifies the cross, and the laver signifies the washing of the Holy Spirit. This is the experience of salvation. In the Holy Place are the showbread table, the golden lampstand, and the incense altar, signifying the bread of life, the light of life, and the fragrance of resurrection respectively. Finally, there is the Holy of Holies, in which is only one item—the ark. We all know that the ark signifies Christ. The ark is in the Holy of Holies; this means that Christ is in our spirit. We are the temple of God, and our spirit is the Holy of Holies. The Lord is not in our soul but in our spirit. Therefore, to enter into the Holy of Holies is to turn to our spirit. To come forward to the throne of grace is to come before the Christ who is in our spirit. God dispenses grace to man, meets with man, and fellowships with man at the throne of grace, that is, in Christ.

There are some believers who believe that, according to Hebrews chapters eight and nine, the Holy of Holies signifies heaven, where the Lord is today. This is correct. However, today the Holy of Holies is also our spirit. If the Holy of Holies refers only to heaven, how can we enter it? Verse 19 of chapter ten explicitly says that we have the boldness to enter the Holy of Holies. Dear brothers and sisters, it is true that the Holy of Holies is in heaven, but because of the eternal Spirit, the Holy of Holies in heaven has been brought into our spirit. Today we do not need to go to heaven to contact the Lord; we just need to turn to our spirit. Let us use electricity as an illustration. Electricity is at the power plant, but today it has been transmitted into the house. Today when we want to use electricity, we do not need to go to the power plant; we can use it right where we are. Thus, subjectively speaking, today our spirit is the Holy of Holies. The Holy of Holies within us and the Holy of Holies in heaven are connected. If the eternal Spirit were not in us, then the Holy of Holies in the heavens would not be connected to us within. Since the eternal Spirit is in us, He connects the Holy of Holies in heaven to our spirit. As a result, our spirit has become the Lord's Holy of Holies. We can enter the Holy of Holies at any time and anywhere. This is to turn to our spirit. To come to the throne of grace is to come forward to Christ, to contact God and touch God in Christ. Today the speaking Spirit, who is also the Spirit as our enjoyment and the unlimited, eternal Spirit, is in our spirit. Therefore, our spirit is the Holy of Holies, and the Lord is with us in our spirit. Hence, for us to draw near to the Lord, to contact the Lord, we must turn to our spirit. However, there is not one Christian who has thoroughly learned this lesson. Every one of us is still lacking in this matter.

Brothers and sisters, when you are saved by receiving the Lord as your Savior, you enjoy the redemption of the Lamb and also receive the washing of the Holy Spirit, yet all of this belongs to the outer court. Gradually, you go one step further and know how to enjoy the Lord as life, to have the light of life within, and to enjoy the fragrance of the Lord's resurrection. You may feel that this is very good. However, you must remember that all of this is still in the Holy Place, in the soul. When I was young, I do not know how often I heard messages of appreciation for the blessing that the Israelites had in eating the manna. Finally one day, I saw that although manna was good, it was eaten in the wilderness. When the Israelites entered Canaan, they ceased eating manna. Thus, although manna is good, it is prepared for the saints who are wandering in the wilderness. Once you enter Canaan and know how to labor together with God on the land in Canaan to bring forth produce from the land, then you will no longer need the manna. Therefore, manna is for the childish Christians, the wandering Christians, and the Christians who are still living in their soul. Once you enter into Canaan, the Holy of Holies, the land of rest, and you truly know how to co-labor with God, at that time the Christ whom you enjoy will no longer be manna to you. If He is manna, He is not merely the manna that came down from heaven. Rather, He is the hidden manna, which is much deeper.

Dear brothers and sisters, learn to enter into the Holy of Holies to touch the throne of grace. Today many brothers and sisters are still living in their soul. If they turn to their spirit, it is only a moment before they come out of their spirit. For example, a husband and a wife who are believers in the Lord may argue at times over certain trivial matters. Please consider, when they are arguing, are they running out or entering in? Sisters, do not blame me for saying that in general the sisters are more skillful than the brothers in arguing. When a couple argues, eight out of ten times, the husband loses. Therefore, I ask the sisters, when you are arguing, are you entering in or running out? As a matter of fact, you are running out. The more you argue, the more you are outside. The more you argue, the more reasons you have, and there is no end to your reasons. Eventually, your emotion is stirred up, and your will also joins in. Occasionally this may even result in fights. At times a sister may feel that she has been wronged, so she goes to the elders to bring a charge against her husband. When I was in North China, I was involved a great deal in taking care of the affairs of the local church, so I often encountered this kind of thing. Sometimes a sister came to me and said, "Brother Lee, look at your brother...." At that time, because I was still young, I did not have a good understanding of these things, so I often tried to counsel the sister. Little did I know that the more I counseled her, the more her whole being turned to go out, to the extent that even my whole being also went outside. Consequently, there was nothing that I could do, and everything became a mess. Slowly I began to find the secret; I realized that the best way was not to say anything to her, not to give her any advice, and not to reason with her, but to help her pray. Once we prayed together, her being, which had turned outward, began to turn inward. Sometimes she began to weep just by calling, "O Lord." This happened quite often. Why did it happen? It was because she had turned back to her spirit. Once she did that, she entered the Holy of Holies and touched the throne of grace to receive mercy and obtain grace for timely help. Then, out of such a place living waters flowed forth to solve all her problems. This surpassed any amount of human speaking. This is the secret of Christian living.

For this reason, Hebrews speaks about discerning the spirit and entering into the Holy of Holies. If you do not discern the spirit, you are in the soul and not in the Holy of Holies. Brothers and sisters, the secret of Christian living is absolutely not a matter of dealing with anything outwardly but a matter of returning to the spirit to enter into the Holy of Holies, to come before the throne of grace, where there is mercy and grace flowing forth as living waters to transform us from within. A Christian is not one who has been changed on the outside but one who has been transformed on the inside. Today there is truly a great mystery within us. In these recent years, having been led by the Lord to pay attention particularly to the matter of the spirit, I sense that it is truly mysterious. The Spirit, as the speaking Spirit, the Spirit of grace, and the unlimited, eternal Spirit, is right within our spirit, making our spirit God's Holy of Holies. The Christ who lives in us is the throne of grace as the base, the ground, for the dispensing of grace. In Him, God is pleased to dispense grace to us. Once you turn to the spirit, you meet Christ and God; grace and mercy flow as living waters within you. Then all of your problems are solved.

Therefore, I repeat, brothers and sisters, where is the key to the book of Hebrews? It is in the Holy of Holies, and this Holy of Holies is your spirit. The key to this book is in 4:12; that is, we need to discern the spirit from the soul. Now you understand why this matter is mentioned only in this Epistle and not in the other Epistles. This book shows us that the exodus from Egypt of the children of Israel in the Old Testament and their wandering in the wilderness is a type. The New Testament believers may be just like them, wandering outside of the Holy of Holies and never entering into the rest to enjoy Christ. Today the good land is Christ, who is in our spirit. If we do not turn to the spirit, we will be wandering in the wilderness of our soul and not entering into the rest. If you read 4:9-12, you will know that there is a rest that remains for us. We must be diligent to enter into that rest. The word of God is living and is able to divide our spirit from our soul. It is thus that we are able to enter into the rest. For this reason, these verses say that you must divide the spirit from the soul and that you must not remain in the soul. If you remain in the soul, you are still wandering in the wilderness and are unable to enter into rest.

Brothers and sisters, do you see how great this grace is? In the Old Testament, only the High Priest could enter into the Holy of Holies, but today every saved person can enter into the Holy of Holies. However, this depends on your decision. If you remain in the outer court, you are only a Levite. If you reach only the Holy Place, you are only a priest. If you turn to the spirit, to contact the Lord Himself directly, then you are a high priest. Whether you are a Levite, a priest, or a high priest depends on you. The Lord's desire is that you be a high priest. He desires that you enter into the Holy of Holies, to come forward to the throne of grace, to receive mercy and obtain grace for timely help. Satan's strategy is to continuously tempt us to go outside. Once you are outside, you are defeated; you have fallen into Satan's deception. However, once you turn to the spirit, you can overcome, you are in the heavens, and you are in the Lord's Holy of Holies. Christ is with you, and once you touch His throne of grace, His mercy and grace will flow as the living waters to water you continually within. This is something that the unbelievers do not understand. This truly is tremendous grace. If you truly touch this, you will have no unresolved problems. Every problem will automatically be solved.

CHAPTER ELEVEN

JAMES THROUGH JUDE

JAMES—THE SPIRIT OF ENVY

Or do you think that the Scripture says in vain: "The Spirit, whom He has caused to dwell in us, longs to envy"? (James 4:5)

Bible readers have had many arguments about this verse in James. Some think that the entire verse is one sentence, while others maintain that it is composed of two sentences, as shown in the following rendering: "Or think ye that the scripture speaketh in vain? Doth the spirit which he made to dwell in us long unto envying?" (ASV). According to the thought of the entire book and the immediate context, we agree that it is one sentence, as shown in the paragraph above. The Spirit who dwells in us longs for us to love God and to turn toward Him to such an extent that He has an envying heart inside us. The four preceding verses tell us that as corrupted men, we easily incline toward the world, love the world, and become joined to the world until we have an illicit union with the world and become adulteresses before God. However, the Spirit of God who indwells us longs for us to love God and be single-heartedly focused on Him. This longing causes Him even to envy over us. The meaning of this envying is like that spoken of in Exodus 20, which says that God is a jealous God. *Jealous* there means *envious*. God is a God of envy. In 2 Corinthians 11 the apostle Paul also said the same thing. He said, "I am jealous over you with a jealousy of God; for I betrothed you to one husband to present you as a pure virgin to Christ. But I fear lest somehow...your thoughts would be corrupted from the simplicity and the purity toward Christ" (vv. 2-3). This portion also says that God has a jealous heart, an envying heart, toward us because He wants us to be solely for Him and to turn toward Him. He does not want us to have any other love apart from Him, just as a husband desires his wife to love him and wants his wife to be only for him.

The book of James talks about how we should have a godly living, a God-like living. In such a living, the first requirement is that we love God absolutely just as a wife loves her husband absolutely. The husband's unique desire with respect to his wife is that she would be absolutely for him. If the wife has any love other than her husband, that will stir up his jealousy. The indwelling Spirit of life in us is the jealous God. He will not permit or allow us to have any love apart from Him. If we have any love apart from Him, it will arouse His jealousy. Thus, it says here that the Spirit, whom God has caused to dwell in us, longs to envy.

"Do you think that the Scripture says in vain?" Where was this word spoken in the Old Testament? You cannot find it anywhere in the Old Testament, but the entire Old Testament definitely reveals such a thought. For example, the books of Isaiah, Jeremiah, Ezekiel, and Hosea all contain this thought. These four books all give us a deep feeling that God is the Husband to the children of Israel. In these four books, God tells the children of Israel that they were wedded to Him as a wife, but they were not faithful to Him. His love toward them was a jealous love. The general summary of these four books is that God longs for us to the extent of being envious.

We know this from our experience also. The indwelling Holy Spirit in us longs for us to love God, to be for God, and to pursue the Lord. When we love someone or something apart from the Lord, we can feel that in the deepest part of our being there is a story of envy, a story of jealousy. That is the story of the indwelling Holy Spirit longing to envy. Therefore, the indwelling Spirit referred to in James can be called the Spirit of envy.

This book has another verse which speaks of the opposite aspect of the Spirit. Verse 15 of chapter three says, "This wisdom is not that which descends from above, but is earthly, soulish, demonic." You see that *soulish* is connected to *earthly* and *demonic*. Therefore, we must know that whenever we are living in the soul, we are joined to the earth and connected to demons. It says here that this kind of wisdom causes us to have bitter jealousy and selfish ambition and is not the wisdom that descends from above, but is earthly, soulish, demonic. If we do not live in the spirit, we are living in the soul. The soulish man, however, is earthly and demonic. This is a very serious matter.

FIRST PETER—THE SPIRIT OF GLORY

First Peter has more references to the indwelling Spirit.

The Sanctifying Spirit

Chosen according to the foreknowledge of God the Father in the sanctification of the Spirit unto the obedience and sprinkling of the blood of Jesus Christ: Grace to you and peace be multiplied. (1 Pet. 1:2)

We have a story inside us which is the story of sanctification. This story of sanctification is the work of the Holy One, the Spirit, in our spirit to separate us, to make us holy. Thus, the sanctification of the Spirit is the work of the Spirit of God, the Holy One, in our spirit to continually separate us from all things that are opposed to God and to continually work the element of God into us, enabling us to become holy. In the sanctification of the Spirit we are able to obey the Lord.

The Spirit of Christ

Concerning this salvation the prophets, who prophesied concerning the grace that was to come unto you, sought and searched diligently, searching into what time or what manner of time the Spirit of Christ in them was making clear. (vv. 10-11)

Prophets here refers to the Old Testament prophets. You might ask, how could the Spirit of Christ be in the Old Testament? We need to add a word of explanation here. According to what we have said in the past, first there was the Spirit of God, then the Spirit of Jesus, and finally the Spirit of Christ; this is with regard to His process. But in another aspect, this Spirit is also timeless, just as the cross is. The crucifixion was accomplished two thousand years ago, but its efficacy is eternal, not being subject to time. In the same way, according to the process of completion, this Spirit was originally the Spirit of God; at the time of the incarnation He was the Holy Spirit, that is, "the Spirit the Holy"; and after passing through death and resurrection, He is the life-giving Spirit, the Spirit of Jesus Christ. According to His efficacy, however, He is the eternal Spirit. Therefore, even in the Old Testament, the Spirit of Christ was in the prophets to enable them to understand the prophecies concerning Christ. The Spirit of Christ testified beforehand to the prophets, making clear to them the time and the manner of time concerning the sufferings and glories of Christ.

A Spiritual House

You yourselves also, as living stones, are being built up as a spiritual house into a holy priesthood to offer up spiritual sacrifices acceptable to God through Jesus Christ. (2:5)

This building is spiritual, and the sacrifices offered are also spiritual. This tells us two things. First, our being built up together is a matter in spirit. When you are in spirit, I am in spirit, and everyone is in spirit, then there is the possibility of our being built up together. The last verse in Ephesians 2 says, "In whom you also are being built together into a dwelling place of God in spirit." The church's being built up into a house is a matter in the spirit. As living stones, we are built up together in spirit, so we become a spiritual house. Second, this building is a priesthood. In this priesthood we are able to have the proper service and offer up spiritual sacrifices. Thus, the building up is in spirit, and the service is also in spirit. The building up and the service should both be in spirit. Furthermore, these two matters are actually two sides of one thing.

The Hidden Man

But the hidden man of the heart in the incorruptible adornment of a meek and quiet spirit. (3:4)

This is a very particular passage in the entire New Testament. No other passage contains such words. In the phrase *the hidden man of the heart,* the word *heart* is a weighty, not empty, term. The three parts of the soul—mind, emotion, and will—plus the conscience, which is a part of the spirit, make up the heart. Here the hidden man of the heart is the regenerated spirit. The inner man is hidden in the heart, and the heart surrounds the spirit. This man should have an adornment, which is a meek and quiet spirit.

This shows us two things. First, our spirit is a hidden man in our heart. Second, our spirit is surrounded by our heart, so our spirit becomes the source in the depths of our heart. The deep source of the mind, emotion, and will is the spirit. Therefore, if you want your mind, emotion, and will to be proper, you must deal with them from the source, from your spirit in your deepest part. This is why your spirit must be meek and quiet. When your spirit is meek and quiet, it is easy for your mind, emotion, and will to be meek and quiet. Many times when you cannot quiet down, it is not a matter involving your mind, emotion, or will; rather, it is because your spirit is in turmoil. When the center is in turmoil, it affects also the surrounding parts. When the source is in turmoil, it affects also the mind, the emotion, and the will. We all know that when our spirit is agitated, our mind, emotion, and will are easily excited and are difficult to calm down. Therefore, I repeat, we need to pray in spirit that our spirit may be quieted, and in this way our mind, emotion, and will also become restful and quieted.

The Spirit of Glory

If you are reproached in the name of Christ, you are blessed, because the Spirit of glory and of God rests upon you. (4:14)

This verse tells us that the Spirit is of glory, that He is full of glory. Furthermore, the phrase *the Spirit of glory and of God* means that the Spirit of glory is the Spirit of God. When you are persecuted for the Lord, the Spirit of God, who is the Spirit of glory, rests upon you.

What is glory? Glory is God manifested, God expressed. When Stephen was martyred, his face was transfigured to resemble the face of an angel; that was the glory of God being manifested. With the martyrs, usually at the moment they suffered martyrdom, there was a condition showing that God was expressed. That was the Spirit of glory and of God resting upon them.

I can never forget the time more than thirty years ago when I met a fifty-year old brother who was zealously preaching the gospel for the Lord. When I asked him how he had been saved, he said that he was from the Shantung Peninsula. When he was young, he had gone to Talien and stayed in a hotel there. The owner of the hotel was a zealous Christian who preached the gospel to him and brought him to salvation. The owner himself had a special story about his own salvation. He had owned this hotel for sixteen or seventeen years, and prior to that time he had been in Peking learning the business in a certain shop during the year of the Boxer Rebellion. One day there was rioting in the streets, so all the shops were tightly closed. He watched through a crack in the shutters and saw the Boxers carrying swords and marching by. In their midst was a donkey pulling a cart in which a young girl was sitting. It turned out that she was a Christian who had been captured by the Boxers, and they were taking her off to execute her. This girl was singing hymns in the cart. She was not only joyful but also shining. This incident gave the man a deep impression. He said, "I must find out about this. What is the religion of Jesus? What kind of medicine did she take to give her such strength?" Hence, he later went to find a believer in Jesus, heard the gospel, and was saved. My intention in telling this story is to show you that when a person is martyred, persecuted, or reproached for the Lord, the Spirit of glory rests upon him.

If we put together the verses above, we see that the Epistles of 1 and 2 Peter emphasize the Spirit of glory. These Epistles speak about how, when Christians suffer for the Lord, the Spirit of Christ rests upon them to express and release God from within them. When people suffer for a worldly matter, they are troubled so much that they always have a sad or distressed expression and are unable to get through. However, Christians are not like this because the indwelling Spirit, who is also the Spirit of glory, rests upon them to manifest the glory of God.

FIRST JOHN—THE ANOINTING SPIRIT

Now let us come to 1 John. The Holy Spirit mentioned in 1 John has a special place in the Bible. The most important verse is the following:

The anointing which you have received from Him abides in you, and you have no need that anyone teach you; but as His anointing teaches you concerning all things and is true and is not a lie, and even as it has taught you, abide in Him. (2:27)

The anointing mentioned here refers to the Holy Spirit. This anointing is constantly moving and working within us. The purpose of this moving is to add the element of God into us. The element of God is like paint, and the moving of the Holy Spirit within us is like someone painting a piece of furniture. We understand God's will and God's leading not by an explicit word in letters but through the inward anointing. For example, I may be a painter painting a room, and you may ask me what color I am painting it. I do not answer you with words; instead, I simply apply some paint on the walls and you know as soon as you see it. Today the inward moving and anointing of the Holy Spirit causes us to have more of the element of God. When God's element increases, we understand more of what God wants, and we are clearer about God's leading.

The Spirit of Mutual Abiding

And he who keeps His commandments abides in Him, and He in him. And in this we know that He abides in us, by the Spirit whom He gave to us. (3:24)

This tells us that we and God, God and we, mutually abide in one another and that this mutual abiding is a matter in the Spirit. God abides in us, and we abide in God. It is not a one-sided matter. Rather, it is two-sided, a kind of mutual abiding that is dependent upon the Spirit whom God gave to us. It is only in this Spirit that we can abide in God and God can abide in us.

In this we know that we abide in Him and He in us, that He has given to us of His Spirit. (4:13)

This is still a mutual abiding. This mutual abiding is altogether a story in spirit. When God abides in us, He abides in our spirit; when we abide in God, we abide in His Spirit.

The Testifying Spirit

The Spirit is He who testifies, because the Spirit is the reality. For there are three who testify, the Spirit and the water and the blood, and the three are unto the one thing. (5:6b-8)

The Spirit here refers mainly to the Spirit in the Lord's incarnation. The water here refers mainly to the water of the Lord Jesus' baptism. The blood here refers mainly to the blood shed through the Lord Jesus' death. Therefore, in this portion John spoke of the Lord Jesus' birth, baptism, and death because these three things testify that the Lord Jesus is the Son of God.

When the Lord Jesus was born in the flesh, the Holy Spirit came upon Mary so that the holy thing which she bore was called the Son of God. Then, when the Lord Jesus was baptized in the water, as He came up from the water, there was a voice saying, "This is My beloved Son." Furthermore, when the Lord Jesus died on the cross and shed His blood, the centurion also testified and said, "Truly this was the Son of God." Regardless of whether it was His birth, His baptism, or His death, they all testified that He is the Son of God. The birth, the baptism, and the crucifixion of the Lord Jesus were special. When the Lord Jesus was on the earth, these three great things testified that He is the Son of God.

This passage shows us that the indwelling Spirit is also the testifying Spirit. Therefore, the indwelling Spirit spoken of in this book functions in three aspects. First, He causes us to have a mutual abiding with God; we abide in God and God abides in us through this Spirit. Second, He testifies within us. Third, He anoints us inwardly. Simply speaking, the Spirit mentioned in this book is the anointing Spirit. This anointing Spirit causes us to have a mutual abiding with God and testifies in us for the Lord Jesus.

There is no mention of the Spirit in 2 and 3 John, so we will skip over them.

JUDE—THE PRAYING SPIRIT

But you, beloved, building up yourselves upon your most holy faith, praying in the Holy Spirit. (Jude 20)

This verse tells us that the Spirit who is in us is a praying Spirit, so our prayer must also be in this indwelling Spirit.

In contrast, verse 19 says, "These are those who make divisions, soulish, having no spirit." Those who have no spirit are those whose spirits are deadened and have become useless. They are soulish, living in the soul, and walking according to the soul, so their spirits cannot be seen in them or in their living and actions. This does not mean that they do not have a spirit within them. Rather, it means that they do not appear to be those who have a spirit. We, however, must pray in spirit. Today this praying Spirit is abiding in your spirit, so you must live in spirit. Thus, the Spirit in Jude is the praying Spirit.

You see that the Epistles of Paul, James, Peter, John, and Jude all speak about the Spirit. These were the only five men who wrote the Epistles, and they all spoke about this Spirit. By this you can realize how important this matter is. Even Jude, who wrote only one chapter, still emphatically mentioned that we need to pray in the Spirit and not be one who lives merely in the soul without using the spirit. May God truly enlighten us until we, too, consider this matter to be as important as they did.

CHAPTER TWELVE

REVELATION

THE REVEALING SPIRIT

I was in spirit on the Lord's Day and heard behind me a loud voice like a trumpet. (Rev. 1:10)

Immediately I was in spirit; and behold, there was a throne set in heaven, and upon the throne there was One sitting. (4:2)

And one of the seven angels who had the seven bowls came and spoke with me, saying, Come here; I will show you the judgment of the great harlot who sits upon the many waters.... And he carried me away in spirit into a wilderness; and I saw a woman sitting upon a scarlet beast, full of names of blasphemy, having seven heads and ten horns. (17:1, 3)

And one of the seven angels who had the seven bowls full of the seven last plagues came and spoke with me, saying, Come here; I will show you the bride, the wife of the Lamb. And he carried me away in spirit onto a great and high mountain and showed me the holy city, Jerusalem, coming down out of heaven from God. (21:9-10)

Please pay attention to the fact that the four passages quoted above all say the writer was "in spirit." We must know that the visions or revelations in the book of Revelation are shown in these four times of being "in spirit." The first time the apostle John was in spirit he saw the seven golden lampstands and the Lord who walks in the midst of them. This is the vision in the first three chapters of Revelation. The second time, he saw a throne in heaven out of which the seven seals, seven trumpets, and seven bowls were executed. This is the vision of the throne, which is in chapters four through sixteen. The third time, he saw Babylon the harlot, which is in chapters seventeen and eighteen and which includes also chapters nineteen and twenty. The fourth time, he saw the New Jerusalem. This is in chapters twenty-one and twenty-two. Revelation can be divided into four sections, covering four great visions, all of which were seen by John in spirit. Therefore, today if we want to understand these four visions in Revelation, we cannot merely read about them in our mind; instead, we must exercise to turn to our spirit. In Revelation you see that the indwelling Spirit is the revealing Spirit.

THE SPEAKING SPIRIT

> To the messenger of the church in Ephesus write: These things says He who holds the seven stars in His right hand, He who walks in the midst of the seven golden lampstands.... He who has an ear, let him hear what the Spirit says to the churches. (2:1, 7a)

Each of the seven epistles in Revelation 2 and 3 begins by saying that it is the Lord who speaks and ends by saying that everyone who has an ear should hear what the Spirit says to the churches. This tells us that the Lord's speaking is the Spirit's speaking, and it also tells us that whatever the Lord speaks must be spoken again by the Spirit. At the beginning of each of the seven epistles it is the Lord speaking to a particular church, but at the end it is the Spirit speaking to the churches. The Lord's word at the beginning is to a certain local church, but later when the people from all the ages read it, it becomes the Spirit's speaking to all the churches. Whatever the Lord speaks is recorded in the Bible, but when you and I read it, the Spirit still must speak it. (This Spirit refers to the Spirit who is mingled with us.) This matter proves firstly that the Lord's speaking is the Spirit's speaking and that the Spirit's speaking is the Lord's speaking. Secondly, it proves that although the Lord's word was already spoken to a certain local church, today when the churches want to hear His word, there is still the need for the Spirit to speak it. This tells us that the Spirit we have within us is not only the revealing Spirit, the vision-imparting Spirit, but also the speaking Spirit.

THE ADMINISTRATING SPIRIT

Now let us look at the third aspect. In chapter four, at the beginning it says that there was a throne set in heaven, and upon the throne was God. Then verse 5 says:

> Out of the throne come forth lightnings and voices and thunders. And there were seven lamps of fire burning before the throne, which are the seven Spirits of God. (4:5)

The seven Spirits are the seven lamps of fire.

> And I saw in the midst of the throne and of the four living creatures and in the midst of the elders a Lamb standing as having just been slain, having seven horns and seven eyes, which are the seven Spirits of God sent forth into all the earth. (5:6)

It says here that the seven Spirits of God are the seven eyes of the Lamb. The seven Spirits are the seven lamps and the seven eyes; this is truly difficult to understand. Are there really seven Spirits of God? No, there are not. Then why is the Spirit of God called the seven Spirits? In the past the expositors of the Bible all told us that seven is the number of completion. This is correct. For example, the first time the Bible mentions the number seven is after God did the work of creation in six days, when He rested on the seventh day (Gen. 2:2). The Bible also says "a righteous man falls seven times and rises up again" (Prov. 24:16) and "seven times a day I praise You" (Psa. 119:164). These passages all have the meaning of completion. However, in the book of Revelation seven denotes not only completion but, even more, God's administration.

The book of Revelation covers mainly four major topics: the first major topic is the seven golden lampstands, the second major topic is the seven seals, the third major topic is the seven trumpets, and the fourth major topic is the seven bowls. Revelation speaks mainly about these four sevens. The seven golden lampstands are the churches. Apart from the churches there are the seven seals which speak of God's judgments throughout the ages. The seven trumpets include the seven bowls, which are God's final judgments. Therefore, the seven seals, seven trumpets, and seven bowls are all God's judgment, and God's judgment is His administration. Not only so, even the seven golden lampstands, that is, even the churches, are God's administration. When God carries out His will in the universe, that is His administration. Some people say that the book of Revelation is a book about judgment. They are right because the Lord is first in the midst of the lampstands judging the seven churches, then later through the seven seals, seven trumpets, and seven bowls, He judges the world. However, you should remember that the judgment of God is the procedure by which He carries out His will, so these judgments are all God's administration. Thus, in the book of Revelation, the number seven denotes administration more than it denotes completion.

Now we have found the meaning of the seven Spirits. In the book of Revelation the Spirit of God is called the seven Spirits because in this book the Spirit of God is the administrating Spirit. He has been sent out into all the world to administrate, to execute the will of God. With respect to the throne of God, He is the seven lamps of fire burning before the throne and shining on the entire universe. With respect to the Lord Jesus, He is the seven eyes of the Lamb of God. The eyes are for moving. Every time you want to do something, you first move your eyes; without your eyes, you cannot move. Chapter one clearly says that when the Lord Jesus judges the churches, His eyes are like a flame of fire. These eyes as a fiery flame are the lamps of fire.

You see that there is a throne in heaven, and the One who is upon the throne is God. From the throne seven lamps of fire shine forth. These seven lamps of fire are the seven Spirits of God, and these seven Spirits of God are the seven eyes of the Lamb. Thus, you see that the One on the throne and the Lamb are one. If this were not the case, how could the seven lamps of fire on the throne become the seven eyes of the Lamb? When you read chapter twenty-two, you notice that it refers to "the throne of God and of the Lamb" (v. 1b). That throne is not plural but singular. There are two on the throne, but the throne is one. How can two be sitting on one throne? It is possible because God is in the Lamb. Chapter twenty-one says that God is the light of the city, and the Lamb is the lamp

(v. 23). We all know that the light is inside the lamp. This proves that God is in the Lamb. Therefore, They are sitting on one throne.

With regard to the seven lamps before the throne, they are the seven eyes of the Lamb, and these seven eyes are the seven Spirits. In other words, they are God's coming forth and the Lamb's coming forth. These seven eyes are the expression and manifestation of the Lamb, just as your eyes are your expression and manifestation. Thus, here in Revelation it is God on the throne in the Lamb coming forth in His Spirit to execute His will for His administration in the universe. He is not hidden as in the past; He has shined forth. God's administration in the church is His coming forth, and God's administration in the universe is also His coming forth. God's using seven seals to judge the world is His coming forth, His using seven trumpets to judge the world is His coming forth, and His using seven bowls to judge the world is also His coming forth. God's administration is God's coming forth. God's way of coming forth is to shine with the lamps of fire. This shining in Revelation is not so much for giving grace but for observing, searching, and judging.

Brothers and sisters, you should never think that the Lord's shining today is to give you grace. No! Even in the age of God's grace, He is here observing you. God does not wait until the age of grace is over and then judge us in a future age. Even in the church, the manifestation of the Lord Jesus is also for the carrying out of His judgment. His eyes are as a flame of fire, and out of His mouth proceeds a sharp sword rather than the words of grace. Before, in the Gospel of John, the words that came out of the mouth of the Lord Jesus were words of grace. But here in the book of Revelation, the words coming out of the mouth of the Lord Jesus are not words of grace but words of judgment. His two feet are like shining bronze as having been fired in a furnace. He has been tried and judged in all kinds of hardships, and now He comes to observe and judge. This is why John, who could lie on the Lord's breast in the Gospel of John, fell flat on the ground when he saw Him now. At this time He is not the dear and lovely Lord; rather, He is the awesome and dreadful Lord. He is here shining, examining, and judging to execute God's will. This is His administration.

Dear brothers and sisters, nothing of the flesh, of the world, or of sin can stand the shining of the seven Spirits as the seven lamps before the throne and as the seven eyes of the Lamb. This shining is a burning. Whatever He shines on, whatever He searches, is judged and burned by Him. Even today the indwelling Spirit in us is sometimes this kind of shining, searching, judging Spirit. This indwelling Spirit is not only the Spirit of life, the Spirit of sonship, the building Spirit, the transforming Spirit, the Spirit for our living, and the Spirit of the Body, all of which are aspects on the sweet side. Eventually, He is also the judging Spirit, the administrating Spirit, who is in us and among us, shining over us, searching us, judging us, and burning us. We need the grace-giving Spirit, and we also need the judging Spirit. We need the Spirit as the living water flowing in us, but we also need the Spirit as fire shining, searching, judging, and burning in us. This is the seven Spirits in Revelation.

THE PROPHESYING SPIRIT

And I fell before his feet to worship him. And he said to me, Do not do this. I am your fellow slave and a fellow slave of your brothers who have the testimony of Jesus. Worship God. For the testimony of Jesus is the spirit of the prophecy. (19:10)

The administrating Spirit is mainly for prophesying, so the administrating Spirit is also the prophesying Spirit, who is for the testimony of Jesus. You should never think that administration and judgment are only for administration and judgment. No! All of God's administration and judgment are for the testimony of the Lord Jesus. When you receive the enlightenment from the throne, are searched inwardly, and are judged, that is the time the prophesying Spirit testifies for the Lord Jesus. Thus, the administrating Spirit is the prophesying Spirit for the testimony of Christ.

THE GOD OF THE SPIRITS OF THE PROPHETS

And he [the angel] said to me, These words are faithful and true; and the Lord, the God of the spirits of the prophets, has sent His angel to show to His slaves the things which must quickly take place. (22:6)

This tells us that God as our God is in our spirit. He is our God not in our soul but in our spirit. God is Spirit, and as such He is the God in our spirit. He is the God of the spirits of the prophets. If we want to understand the things of God as the prophets do, then we must be in spirit. If we are not in spirit, we cannot have God as our God, nor can we understand the things of God.

THE SPIRIT AND THE CHURCH BEING ONE

The Spirit and the bride say, Come! (22:17)

At the end of Revelation, the Spirit and the church have become one, and they are speaking together. The word spoken by the bride, the church, is the word spoken by the Spirit, and the Spirit speaks through the bride, the church. The Spirit speaks together with the bride.

In summary, the Spirit in Revelation is in six aspects. First, "I was in spirit." Second, the Lord's speaking is the Spirit's speaking, and the Lord's speaking must be repeated by the Spirit. Third, the Spirit of the Lord today is the seven Spirits as the expression of the Lord Himself to enlighten us, search us, judge us, and burn us. Fourth, the Lord as the Spirit is the prophesying Spirit for the testimony of the Lord Jesus. Fifth, God can only be our God in this Spirit, so He is the God of our spirits, the God of the spirits of the prophets. Sixth, the Spirit speaks through the church; the church and the Spirit become one to speak for God. If you put these six aspects together, you can see that today everything hinges on this Spirit. It is by this Spirit that you can see the visions and understand the mysterious things of God. It is by this Spirit that you can hear the words which were already spoken by the Lord. Furthermore, if you are a saved person, then you are certainly one who has first been judged. The seven Spirits of God first come to judge you. The seven Spirits of God are among the seven golden lampstands first judging His church, His household. If we fall behind in being judged, then it proves that we have been disapproved. If we are judged last, we are the disapproved ones; if we are judged first, we are the saved ones. In this way, we have the prophesying Spirit and can testify for the Lord in this Spirit. Then we can touch God as the Spirit in our spirit. God is the God of our spirit. Eventually, the Spirit and we become one. The Spirit speaks out from within us, and our speaking here is by this Spirit.

Therefore, brothers, I feel deeply and believe truly that nothing in the New Testament is more important than the Spirit. However, from times past to the present time, this Spirit has been mostly neglected. Today most people pay attention to the outpouring of the Holy Spirit, while some pay a small amount of attention to the indwelling Spirit, but no one has developed the matter of the indwelling Spirit as much, as richly, or as broadly as we have today. In these past few days what we have studied is just an outline. Following this, you still have to spend time to study the details carefully and pray over them in spirit.

The Lord Jesus said, "It is the Spirit who gives life;...the words which I have spoken to you are spirit and are life" (John 6:63). The words spoken by the Lord to us must be spirit before they can be life. But how can the words spoken to us by the Lord become spirit to us? We must turn them into prayer. You take the word which you have read and understood and turn it into spirit, and it is in spirit that you will see the visions. This is the Spirit's speaking to you. The Lord has already spoken the things in the Bible, but now in the Spirit He will speak them to you. This is when your inward being will truly seem to have seven lamps of fire burning and shining in it. Having been enlightened and searched within, you will see many things that need to be judged. When you are judged in this way, the Spirit in you will become the testifying Spirit, the prophesying Spirit, who is for the testimony of the Lord Jesus. You will also touch the presence of God. At this time the Spirit and you will become one. I hope that we will truly have the practice, exercise, and experience of these matters.

PART TWO

THE SPIRIT IN
THE EPISTLES OF PAUL

THE REALITY OF THE BIBLE BEING IN THE SPIRIT

CHRISTIANITY EMPHASIZING DOCTRINE BUT LACKING THE SPIRIT

I think I need to say an opening word. We all know that Christianity today has fallen into such a condition that it has become a religion. The prerequisites of any religion are beliefs or doctrines and rituals or methods. Therefore, every religion has its doctrines and its rituals. Since Christianity has fallen into religion, it also manifests this kind of condition, having doctrines on the one hand and rituals on the other hand. These two things perfectly fit man's natural concept and taste. Man naturally delights in listening to sermons and watching ceremonies.

The Bible, however, shows us that the Lord's salvation in us is not a religion but altogether a story of life. It is true that we need to have a considerable amount of knowledge about life, but this kind of knowledge is not for knowledge itself; rather, it is for life to exist, to grow, and to become strong. This may be compared to the fact that in today's medical science there is nothing empty; empty theories do not exist in the medical field. Everything in the medical profession is practical, concrete, real, and applicable. Likewise, the words the Lord gives us today are not hollow; rather, they are practical and pragmatic.

However, according to our natural sentiments, we enjoy listening to doctrinal teachings, and we also like performing rituals. Yet these two things are contrary to the Lord's life and have no place in the Bible. Although the Bible covers a great variety of things, strictly speaking, it does not contain the so-called doctrines found in today's Christianity. The Bible is altogether an explanation of life and a guide to life. Moreover, it does not contain any methods or rituals.

From the time of the Reformation with Luther, the reality of redemption has been recovered; there is no question about this. Today no one can take away justification by faith from Christians because this matter has already been recovered into the Christian life. When you read the biographies of the saints in the past, you cannot deny that in the last five hundred years of church history there has been a considerable measure of life. However, we also have to admit that the matter of redemption has gradually been made doctrinal, and the knowledge and experience of life have also been turned into doctrines. Today the situation is that orthodox Christianity has turned many positive things into doctrines. In these recent years some people have made the matters pertaining to the knowledge and experience of life into doctrines, just as theologians made justification by faith into a doctrine. Many of them have the doctrine but not the reality of justification by faith. They have no experience whatsoever of justification by faith, yet they preach the doctrine of justification by faith. They have the belief but not the reality. In the same manner, there are also people who turn the matter of spiritual life into a doctrine. They preach the doctrine concerning life without having the experience of life. Thus, they have made the things pertaining to life into doctrinal matters. As a result, the things of life have nearly become theories, philosophical ideas, and mere teachings.

What is the reason for this? Let me use medical science again as an example. In modern medical science many kinds of vitamins in the food we eat were discovered and thoroughly researched. Hundreds or thousands of years ago our ancestors consumed these vitamins—probably more than we do, but they did not have the knowledge about vitamins. They had the reality but not the knowledge. I am afraid that today some people might have a thorough study of vitamins, yet they might not be taking any vitamins. Thus, you can see that having the knowledge is one thing and having the reality is another thing. The reality of vitamins is in eating and drinking.

You must eat and drink. No matter how much you talk about vitamins, they will be useless to you unless you take them in. In like manner, today we need knowledge, but even more we need reality. What we are afraid of today is that the truths concerning matters such as redemption and life have become doctrines without the reality.

Where is this reality? Dear brothers and sisters, it is in the Spirit. This is the problem of Christianity today. Not to mention those Christians who have fallen into the world or those who are modernists, even those who are fundamental and "spiritual" are lacking in the matter of the Spirit. They do not pay enough attention to the Spirit, nor do they have sufficient experience of the Spirit. What we should know about the Spirit is too little, but compared to the real measure of what we have experienced of the Spirit, what we know is too much. It seems that a great part of what we have consists of knowledge and understanding and that only a small part consists of experience and reality. Therefore, I hope that I can make this matter clear to you and that at the same time I can help you make a proper turn.

THE FOCAL POINT OF THE BIBLE BEING THE SPIRIT

It is not a problem to say that the Bible is a book of doctrines. However, the so-called doctrines in the Bible are not hollow or empty. Rather, biblical truths all serve as explanations and guides, and all impart revelations as well. Therefore, we must not understand the Bible as a book of mere doctrines. What does the Bible explain and reveal? Simply speaking, it shows us that God is the Triune God: that the Father is in the Son, the Son is in the Spirit, and the Spirit as the Triune God reaches us and comes into us to be our life. Therefore, ultimately, the focal point of the entire Bible is that the Triune God as the Spirit comes to be our life.

Furthermore, the entire Bible shows us that man is the center of all God's created things, just as the Chinese sages say that "man is the spirit of all creatures." I have always thought that such a saying is very meaningful. Why is man the spirit of all creatures? It is because among the creatures man is indeed extraordinary and exceedingly wonderful. Man is the center. God did not choose other creatures to be His vessels to contain Him. He only chose man to be united with Him. Furthermore, God did not decide to become any other kind of living being. Rather, He decided to become a man. For this reason, man has a special place in the universe.

Today when the theologians in Christianity talk about man's fall, they emphasize only that man sinned, offended God, lost His blessings, and suffered perdition. They have not seen that the fall of man damaged the vessel which God had created for Himself. God created us to be His vessels. Satan's destruction is to damage us, the vessels of God, so that we are no longer fit to be used by God as His vessels. Therefore, when God comes to redeem and recover us, He not only redeems us from sin and delivers us out of sufferings, but He also recovers us that we may be His vessels again. Furthermore, the focus of His creation and redemption is our spirit. In His creation God created a spirit for us, and in His redemption He restores this spirit of ours. When God regenerates us, He restores the spirit in us.

Thus, we see that the Triune God is Spirit to be received by us and that within us we have a spirit created and regenerated by Him. Hence, there are two spirits. You can find at least three or four verses in the Bible where these two spirits are mentioned together. For instance, the Lord Jesus said, "God is Spirit, and those who worship Him must worship in spirit and truthfulness" (John 4:24). This means that our spirit worships God as Spirit. The Lord also said, "That which is born of the Spirit is spirit" (3:6). The first *Spirit* is God's Spirit, and the second *spirit* is our spirit. Furthermore, Romans 8:16 says, "The Spirit Himself witnesses with our spirit that we are children of God." This verse tells us there are two spirits witnessing together. Then 1 Corinthians 6:17 says, "But he who is joined to the Lord is one spirit." That we can become one spirit with the Lord proves that originally there was not one spirit but two spirits to be joined together.

In the Bible there are at least these four verses showing us the two spirits. Our regeneration and the life we live thereafter, including our overcoming, our being matured, our sanctification, our service, and even the transfiguration of our body in the future, all hinge on the spirit. Therefore, we ought to have adequate knowledge concerning the spirit. We see that the Bible is focused on the spirit and emphatically refers to the spirit. But when we read the Bible, we pay attention to many things other than this matter. This is because the other things are very close to our concepts, while the matter of the spirit is absent from our concept. Therefore, for five hundred years of recovery the attention given to the spirit has still been inadequate. We believe that in these last days God truly will gradually recover this matter. With this as our standpoint, let us now study the New Testament.

THE FOUR GOSPELS SPEAKING ABOUT THE LORD'S BECOMING THE SPIRIT TO BE RECEIVED BY MAN

The first four books of the New Testament are the Gospels. We must worship God that not only do the words in the holy Scriptures contain the revelations of God, but even the arrangement of the books of the Scripture implies God's sovereignty. Take the four Gospels as an example. If you consider their sequence, you will see that it is quite meaningful. Matthew, the first book, opens by telling us that on the one hand, on God's side, Jesus Christ was God begotten in man, and on the other hand, on man's side, He was a descendant brought forth through generations of forefathers. Therefore, at the outset Matthew shows us the genealogy of the Lord, which can be considered almost a sketch of the entire Old Testament. The extract of the entire Old Testament is the genealogy in Matthew chapter one. The Old Testament speaks about the fathers in the past generations inheriting God's promise to bring in a wonderful person; then this wonderful One came. He is God Himself entering into man; He is Emmanuel, God with man. The central point of the Gospel of Matthew is that this One wants to be with us. Therefore, at least three times Matthew refers to the matter of the Lord's being with us. The first time, it mentions Emmanuel, that is, God with us (1:23). Another time, it says, "For where there are two or three gathered into My name, there am I in their midst" (18:20). Still another time, after the Lord's resurrection, it says, "I am with you all the days until the consummation of the age" (28:20). This One is Emmanuel, God mingled with man; as such, He can never be separated from us. Thus, He is with us until the consummation of this age. He is such a One; this is what Matthew shows us.

Next let us look at the two books in the middle, Mark and Luke. They do not speak about God's being with us, nor about Emmanuel. Rather, they show us how this One, who was God with man, the incarnated One, and Emmanuel, lived in man and how He lived out the living of a man. He lived on earth as a real man, and for thirty-three and a half years He lived a real human living on earth. This is what Mark and Luke show us.

Then we come to the Gospel of John. John's emphasis is to show us that this God who was in the beginning came into the world to become a man and then went to the cross. By going to the cross He was transfigured from the flesh into the Spirit. In chapters fourteen through sixteen there is a great turning point, where the Lord was transfigured from the flesh into the Spirit. Once He was transfigured into the Spirit, it became possible for man to live in Him and He in man. He and man were completely joined with one another. This joining, this union, lies with this Spirit. At the end of the Gospel of John, in chapters twenty and twenty-one, this wonderful One was eventually manifested as a breath. This is mysterious to the uttermost. The existence of man hinges on life; the story of man is altogether a story of life. But the matter of life hinges on a breath. Therefore, when a person dies, we say he has expired; that is, he has breathed his last breath. When one breathes his last breath, he is finished, and there is no more life in him. Then what is this breath? This is quite mysterious yet real. The Gospel of John is a record showing that the Triune God is mingled with a descendant who came out of the fathers. Who is this wonderful One? He is the Triune God, the One whose goings forth are from ancient times, from the days of eternity, and who created the universe, mingled with a descendant who came out of the generations of the forefathers. Such a One is too marvelous, and this wonderful One eventually became a breath, which is the Spirit for us to receive. Today when we believe in the gospel, we do not merely believe a doctrine. Rather, we receive a breath. The Lord Jesus in whom we believe is different from any founder of a religion. When one believes in a religion, one believes some teachings or doctrines, but when we believe in the Lord Jesus, we take Him in as a breath.

In the beginning of the four Gospels we see a genealogy in which a descendant was brought in as the issue of the mingling of the Triune God with man. Then at the end of these four books we see that this wonderful One eventually became a breath. He breathed this breath for man to receive the Holy Spirit. He Himself was that breath. As I have said before, in Greek, the word for *breath* is also the word for *spirit*. The Lord Jesus breathed into the disciples and said to them, "Receive the Holy Spirit" (John 20:22). *Receive the Holy Spirit* may well be translated *receive the Holy Breath*. Why is it that when the Lord breathed into the disciples it was for them to receive the Holy Spirit? It is because that Spirit is just the breath. Therefore, ultimately, this wonderful One is this breath. Today when we preach, honestly speaking, we are not only preaching the word to people. Rather, we are transmitting this breath into them through the word. By means of the word we enable others to know, to incline to, and to appreciate this breath. We use the word to introduce this breath to them in order to touch their heart. Thus, after they have been touched, they will not just exercise their mind to agree with and believe in the word, but they will open themselves up entirely to this breath to repent and to pray. This prayer with repentance is a breathing. It is to take in the breath.

Therefore, brothers and sisters, the Christians' proper preaching of the gospel is not just to preach a doctrine. The proper gospel preaching is a story of the spirit. For example, concerning sin, we may be able to give many facts and reasons to prove that human beings are sinful and to eventually convince people to confess that they are sinful. But their confession may be altogether in the mind. It is like someone agreeing that two plus two equals four. This is not the Lord's salvation but human religion. What then is the Lord's salvation? It is that when we speak to someone about sins, in our words there is the spirit which touches the deepest part of his being, causing him not only to admit in his mind that he is sinful but also to groan from deep within, saying, "O Lord, I am a sinner." When he groans, the Lord as the breath enters into him. This is to believe and to be saved from within. To be saved is mainly to inhale the Lord with our spirit, to breathe Him in. When a person hears the gospel and is touched and stirred deep within, he says, "O Lord, forgive me. I have sinned against my father and my mother." Such a confession is actually a breathing. The more he confesses, the more he breathes. Finally, he says, "O Lord, thank You that You died for me on the cross. I want to receive You." The more he prays this way, the more he feels refreshed and peaceful within. This means that the Lord has entered into him as the breath, as the Spirit.

Brothers and sisters, ultimately, this is what the four Gospels speak about. If you recall the four Gospels you read, and if you read them again with a bird's-eye view and from the viewpoint of an abstract, you will see that what they speak about is this: One day the Triune God, who exists from eternity and is the Creator of all things, came into a descendant of many generations of forefathers. In this way God and man were mingled as one entity. Such a One lived on the earth and then finally through death and resurrection He became a breath for man to breathe in and to receive. In essence, this is the four Gospels. It is a pity that previously when we read the four Gospels, all we received from our reading were a great number of teachings, revelations, examples, and stories. Then we went and told others about these things, saying, "See how the Lord Jesus loved the children, how tender He is, how humble He is, how much He suffered, how faithful He is, and how open-hearted He is." All these things are right, but we hardly ever touched the central point, which is that the Lord Jesus became breath for man to breathe in. It is true that when we were speaking about how He was so merciful and so generous, as the Spirit He was also working along with our speaking. However, we must realize that people received help not because of our teachings but because their spirit was opened and was moved and therefore they were able to touch the Spirit of the Lord within.

Therefore, while you are preaching the word, there may be a thousand people listening to you, but only five or six will truly receive help and be saved. The majority of the audience may listen only with their mind, but five or six of them may have a response in their spirit and breathe the Lord in with their spirit. They may forget the words they heard, but they will never forget the fact that they have contacted and gained the Lord within them.

HENCEFORTH, PAYING MORE ATTENTION TO THE SPIRIT THAN TO THE OBJECTIVE WORD

Therefore, dear brothers and sisters, our eyes need to be opened that henceforth, although we should not neglect the word, we must pay more attention to the Spirit. Of course, we need a certain amount of speaking in order to make clear the matter concerning the Spirit, but we absolutely must not speak empty, spiritual theories. Instead, we must pay attention to the reality of the Spirit. From now on, in our service, our work, and our preaching, we must help people to know the Spirit, the breath, and to learn to breathe in more of this breath. I hope that henceforth, among us, we will not take the objective word as our center. When people come into our midst, it should not be for listening to the objective word but for breathing the Lord with their spirit. When people come into our midst, their feeling, inclination, and desire should not be that they come because there are good messages here. Rather, they come because there is fresh air here. Gradually, Christians should have an impression of us that although the messages we preach are good, our focus is not the objective word but the spirit with a spiritual atmosphere. We look to the Lord for His mercy that the churches will all arrive at this goal. In every locality, when the brothers and sisters come together, whether to have a big meeting or a small fellowship, the impression we give others should not be that we are studying the Bible, preaching the word, listening to the preaching, or researching a doctrine. Rather, there should be a certain kind of atmosphere, a certain kind of spirit, that enables others to breathe God and to gain God.

I hope that the brothers and sisters will see that, from now on, in our studying of the word, we should not care too much about studying the doctrines. Instead, we should absorb, breathe in, the Spirit from the word. Every time we release a message, the impression we give people should be the release of the Spirit more than the release of the objective word. From now on, the way of our service should not be like our former way of preaching the word. We still need the preaching of the word, but not all preachings are the same. Until now the emphasis in our preaching has been on the objective word, but from now on it should be on the spirit. Until now our emphasis has been on the speaking, without necessarily releasing the spirit. From now on, however, whenever we open our mouth to speak, there must be the release of the spirit. Moreover, whatever we speak is not hollow, theoretical, or doctrinal. Instead, we should present the real things before others, and in our presentation our spirit must also go forth to touch their spirit. Hence, we must completely change the way of our preaching. In our preaching of the word, we have always put more emphasis on the objective word than on the spirit, but from now on the way we deliver the word should be by the spirit. Our intention should not be for people to listen to a message. Instead, whenever we speak, we should give them an atmosphere of the spirit. They should have the feeling that although we have delivered a good message, the impression we have given them is that our emphasis is not on the objective word but on the spirit.

We hope that from now on the emphasis of our preaching in every locality will not be on giving a message for people to listen to. Instead, our emphasis will be to introduce spiritual life and reality to people through the word and to show them the way to contact this spiritual life and reality so that they can touch it in their spirit. Therefore, we surely must learn to exercise our spirit in our daily life. I say again, pray-reading is most helpful. We must exercise our spirit. In this way, when we speak, instead of speaking empty teachings, we speak the reality which we have experienced, and we also point out this way to people. Furthermore, in all our meetings, including even the meetings for the preaching of the word, there should be sufficient prayer before and after each meeting. We definitely must help the brothers and sisters in the matter of the spirit, and we must avoid being too ritualistic or formal in the meetings. In fact, even if there are over a hundred people in a meeting, there still is no need to have a platform for speaking. Do not be too formal. We must help the brothers and sisters to have an atmosphere in which they pray much and their spirits are living.

Pray-reading started in Taiwan, but it has also been picked up by the church in Los Angeles, and I heard that it is being practiced there even more intensely than here in Taiwan. Recently I received a letter from some of the saints there, telling me that now they no longer preach a message on the Lord's Day morning; instead, it is all pray-reading. They also said that they are even preaching the gospel by pray-reading and that the attendance has increased and many have been saved. Not only so, the practice of pray-reading has a good influence even on the offering of material things.

I am not introducing a method here. What I am saying is that today we must see clearly that in our service to the Lord we cannot rely only on the preaching of the word or on any fixed practice. We ourselves must have good fellowship with the Lord regularly, and our spirit must be living and fresh. This is our capital. Then when we come to any meeting, we should not use any form to bind people. Everyone's spirit must be released so that when people come to our meetings they will be able to touch something that is not a doctrine but the living Spirit. The rituals are gone, yet no one acts disorderly. When people come in, they must touch the spirit. The Lord is with our spirit, and our spirit releases the Lord's Spirit. Although we have the word, the word is simply an explanation that enables people to breathe in and touch the fresh air from heaven. Everyone who comes into our meeting will touch the fresh air. This is something that will help people throughout their entire life.

Chapter Two

THE SPIRIT IN ROMANS

(1)

THE DIFFICULTY IN TOUCHING THE SPIRIT OF THE BIBLE

Many Christians admit that the problem in reading the Bible is that it is relatively easy to find the peripheral things but not very easy to find the central matter. This may be compared to contacting a person; it is hard to perceive the life within him even though it is easy to touch his physical members. We all know that without the physical members it is impossible for the life within to exist. Nevertheless, as far as man is concerned, the physical members are merely the external things; only the life within him is his center. Likewise, the Bible has its spirit, its life, its center. Like a man, the Bible needs a structure with many "members." It has to cover many different matters because without them there is no place in which to put its life and its spirit. The Bible refers to many matters, but these things are not its life, its spirit. Rather, they are a place in which its life, its spirit, may be deposited. Because of this, when a person comes to read the Bible, it is easy for him to find the superficial things, the external things, but not easy to find the spirit within.

THE SPIRIT OF THE GOSPELS BEING THE LORD BECOMING A WONDERFUL SPIRIT

Let us use the Gospels as an example. Many things are written in the Gospels, but actually these four books speak about only this one thing: At His predetermined time, the triune, eternal God, the Creator of all things, entered into the created man to be mingled and united with man; then He lived on earth, and finally He entered into death and came out in resurrection to become a wonderful Spirit. Whatever we need has been accomplished in this Spirit and is included in this Spirit. Today, this wonderful Spirit is like breath; He is very rich and exceedingly available. This is the essence, the spirit, the life, of the Gospels.

Nevertheless, I say again, when you read the four Gospels, you cannot easily discover their essence. You can find many stories in the Gospels, but you cannot easily detect the spirit contained in them. This may be compared to the way a person can be contacted: your ears, hair, eyebrows, hands, and feet can easily be touched, but your life cannot be touched. This is our problem in reading the Bible. Many saints throughout the centuries interpreted the Gospels, but they only talked about the external, superficial things. They did not touch the spirit within.

If we put the four Gospels together and read them with a bird's-eye view in a quiet spirit, then we will see that the life, the essence, the kernel, of these four books is to show us that the Triune God who is in eternity actually entered into the created man to be mingled with man as one, lived the human life, went into death, and in resurrection became the Spirit. Therefore, after His resurrection, He breathed into His disciples and said, "Receive the Holy Spirit."

Please consider again, what do the four Gospels talk about? They do not talk mainly about healing or casting out of demons, nor do they only admonish us to enter into the kingdom of the heavens, nor do they talk about how to have our sins forgiven or how to be born again. I trust that you know what I mean when I say that they do not talk mainly about these things. What then do they talk about? They tell us that one day the Triune God who is in eternity, the Creator of all things, entered into man, lived on this earth, went into death, and became a wonderful Spirit. In this wonderful Spirit there are God, man, redemption, life, holiness, power, light, and love. This Spirit has everything. Therefore, at the end of the Gospels, we are told about a breath. The Triune

God has passed through all the processes and has accomplished everything. Today He is breath.

When Christians read the Gospels, most of them see only that the great God, the Lord of glory, was incarnated to be our Savior, that He shed His precious blood to make atonement for our sins, and that after His death and resurrection, He ascended into the heavens and sat down at the right hand of God. We cannot say that this is wrong, but you must realize that this is not the center or the conclusion of the Gospels. The four Gospels conclude neither with Mark nor with Luke but with John. The Gospel of John does not conclude with ascension. Instead, it concludes with the breathing of a breath for the disciples to receive the Holy Spirit. It was not the Lord ascending to the throne; instead, it was the Lord becoming a breath being breathed into men.

THE SPIRIT IN ROMANS

In the same principle, when you read expositions of the Bible, you can find many commentaries on Romans. We may say that it is rare for any Bible expositor not to write a commentary on Romans. Nearly all Bible teachers have written commentaries on Romans. There are very many expositions of Romans, but it is amazing that you can hardly find one that points out the spirit of Romans. Martin Luther was the first famous writer of a commentary on Romans, although a better publication written by him is his commentary on Galatians, which is his masterpiece. However, whether it is his commentary on Galatians or on Romans, Luther points out only the matter of justification by faith in those two books. It is true that Romans has the matter of justification by faith, just as you have two big shoulders, but these two big shoulders of yours are not the life within you. Justification by faith surely is a great item in the book of Romans, but it is not the soul of the book of Romans. The soul of Romans is spirit and life.

Although the book of Romans has a very specific line with a very focused train of thought, you still can find many peripheral matters that are necessary in order to provide a background for the central matter. However, these peripheral things have become veils that prevent Bible readers from seeing the spirit, the life, of the book. Therefore, when we come to read the Word, we should learn not to be hindered by the peripheral things. Instead, we should penetrate the peripheral things to see the life and the spirit within. This is how we will study Romans now. We will simply point out the crucial matters.

Christ's Designation as the Son of God Being in the Spirit

The first place in Romans that mentions the Spirit, or spirit, is chapter one. The first four verses of chapter one say that the gospel promised by God in previous generations is Jesus Christ, who is of two aspects according to His divinity and His humanity respectively. According to His humanity, He was the seed of David; according to His divinity, He was the Son of God. However, this matter of His being the Son of God was confirmed by the Spirit of holiness; this Spirit confirmed that He was the Son of God. Therefore, you see that in its introduction Romans points out this Spirit. Christ Jesus, who is the subject, content, and center of the gospel, was the seed of David according to His humanity and the Son of God according to His divinity, which is altogether a matter in the Spirit.

Paul Serving God in Spirit

The second place that mentions the spirit is also in chapter one. Verse 9 says that Paul served God in his spirit. The spirit mentioned in the first place is the Spirit of God, whereas the spirit mentioned here in the second place refers to Paul's spirit. Before he was saved, Paul served God in letter, but now he served God in spirit.

Service Being in Spirit and Not in Letter

The third place that mentions the spirit is at the end of chapter two. There it says that what God wants is not the outward service in form and letter but the inward service in spirit. Service is a matter in spirit, not in letter (v. 29).

Dear brothers and sisters, why is it that at the very beginning of this book—which to Martin Luther was a book on justification by faith—it says that Jesus Christ, who is the subject and content of the gospel, is in the Spirit? And why does it say that we should serve God in our spirit and that our service today is not in letter but in spirit? Please remember that the spirit at the end of chapter two is hard to explain. It is clear that 1:4 refers to the Spirit of God, and it is equally clear that 1:9 refers to the spirit of man. But what is the spirit mentioned in 2:29 where it says "in spirit, not in letter"? This is hard to say; no one can explain this. Therefore, eventually we just have to accept the fact that this is the mingled spirit, which is the mingling of two spirits. It is the Spirit of God as well as the spirit of man, and it is the spirit of man as well as the Spirit of God.

What does Romans speak about? If you ask Luther, he would say that it is about justification by faith. Some people might tell you that the first section of Romans is about justification by faith, and the latter section is about sanctification, and that it is here that we need to be in spirit. Why then at the beginning of the first half of Romans is the spirit already mentioned? This implies that what the book of Romans covers is altogether the story of the spirit. The gospel of God is the story of the spirit, service to God is the story of the spirit, and every experience we have before God is a story of the spirit.

The Holy Spirit Pouring Out
the Redemptive Love in Us

After referring to the spirit in 2:29, Romans contains a long section to cover the matter of redemption. Since God could not do anything with fallen man, He had to do the work of redemption first. However, redemption is neither God's central thought nor His final goal. Redemption is simply His procedure. After speaking about redemption, Romans says in the beginning of chapter five that the Spirit of God has poured out His great redemptive love in our hearts. Here it comes back to the Spirit. No doubt, it seems that redemption is a matter outside of us; it is a matter accomplished for us by God outside of us. However, the love of redemption, the feeling of redemption, and our reaction toward redemption still need to be wrought into us, and this can be done only by the Spirit of God. Because the Spirit of God has poured out the redemptive love in us, we have a very subjective response to God's redemption and have a feeling and sentiment toward it. Therefore, the redemptive love comes into us through the Spirit.

Being Saved in His Life

In 5:11 Paul speaks a word which Bible readers have not paid much attention to. In fact, it has been neglected by many. He says that we "rejoice in God through our Lord Jesus Christ, through whom we have now received the reconciliation" (ASV). The word *rejoice* in Greek means to glory or to boast, and it also implies enjoyment. To rejoice in God is to have God as our boast, our glory, and our enjoyment. To have God as our boast is objective, whereas to take God as our enjoyment is subjective. Therefore, what this verse means is that now through the redemption of Christ we can enjoy God, taking God as our enjoyment; hence, God is our joy. The first half of Romans, which is also the first major part, ends with rejoicing in God, boasting in God, and taking God as our enjoyment.

However, the book of Romans does not end at 5:11 with redemption. Instead, it makes a big turn here. As I said before, in Romans there are three big terms, which also represent three major sections. The first section deals with redemption, the second section deals with life, and the third section deals with the Body. Redemption is for life, and life is for the Body. In the verses up to 5:11 redemption is dealt with; from 5:12 to the end of chapter eight life is dealt with. God wants to be your enjoyment and your joy, but how can this be accomplished? This requires that God be your life. When God lives in you, you live by God, and God becomes your life in reality. Then and only then will you truly enjoy God. This is why Paul begins to introduce the word *life* in 5:10.

Romans 5:10 contains the chief point of the book of Romans. There it mentions the death of Christ and the life of Christ. The death of Christ reconciles us to God, whereas the life of Christ saves us subjectively. This subjective salvation, which is a salvation of life, includes five great items: release, sanctification, transformation, conformation, and coordination. This is the subjective salvation which God gives us by being life in us. To be released is to be set free from sins; to be sanctified is to be separated from our naturalness and from the world; to be transformed is to be freed from our old creation; to be conformed is to be shaped into the image of God's Son; and to be coordinated is to become one Body by being delivered from our independence. These thoughts are all there in chapters six, eight, and twelve of Romans. Romans 5:10 says that since we were reconciled to God through the death of God's Son, much more we will be saved in His life. This salvation is not a salvation in the past but a salvation from now on. Furthermore, this salvation is not objective but subjective; it is not the blood but the life that saves us.

This can be seen in the type of the Passover in the Old Testament. The shedding of the blood of the Passover lamb was an objective salvation, while the flesh of the lamb eaten by the children of Israel became their subjective salvation. The blood of the lamb enabled the children of Israel to escape God's condemnation, that is, to be saved out of God's condemnation, whereas the flesh of the lamb gave them the strength to go out of Egypt. We all know that the lamb typifies the Lord Jesus. Therefore, the Lord Jesus said that His flesh is edible. This is life, and this life saves us subjectively.

Reigning in Life

Therefore, the matter of redemption completely ends with 5:11. Actually, it ends with verse 9; from verse 10 there is a turn from the Lord's redemption to life. Verse 11 says that since we have been reconciled to God, we are now enjoying God, and God has become our enjoyment. How can God become our enjoyment? He becomes our enjoyment in the way of life. This is also our salvation. Therefore, the second half of chapter five begins to deal with the matter of life, even to such an extent that it says that we are reigning in life. We have not only been freed and sanctified, but we are even reigning.

Everything that is contrary to or against God has been swallowed by life, and we are able to reign in life.

Living in Newness of Life

Concerning the matter of life, Romans first says in 5:10 that we will be saved in the life of God's Son, and in 5:17 it says that we will reign in life. Then in 6:4 it says that we have died and have been buried with Christ that we may walk in newness of life. Now life has become a living in newness. You can speak a great deal about death, burial, and resurrection, which are all mentioned in Romans 6, but they are all matters outside of you and have nothing to do with you unless you are in Christ's life. It is only when you are in this life that death, burial, and resurrection can become your subjective experience. Therefore, many people have told others strongly, "You have died with Christ, you have been buried with Christ, and you have resurrected with Christ," and they were able to make others understand these matters. Eventually, however, because what they taught were mere doctrines, those who listened to them did not experience death, burial, or resurrection. You need to bring people into Christ as life. Once they live in this life, then spontaneously they will die, be buried, and be resurrected. The reality of death, burial, and resurrection is in life. One must live in Christ as life to have the experience of death, burial, and resurrection in reality.

Serving in Newness of Spirit

In chapter seven, once again the spirit is mentioned. It says that today we should serve the Lord in newness of spirit (v. 6). Chapter six mentions the newness of life, while chapter seven mentions the newness of spirit. These two chapters are a good match. Chapter six concerns our living, while chapter seven concerns our service. Our living should be in newness of life, while our service should be in newness of spirit. I hope, brothers and sisters, that you can remember these two kinds of newness: one is newness of life and the other is newness of spirit. Newness of spirit is for our service, whereas newness of life is for our living. There should be no oldness in either our service and in our living. Concerning our living, we should have the newness of life instead of the oldness of the flesh. Concerning our service, we should have the newness of spirit instead of the oldness of law and letter.

I strongly feel that the brothers who minister the word must see clearly that they need to speak more about these matters. They should release messages to show people what the oldness of the flesh, the newness of life in our living, the oldness of letter, and the newness in spirit in our service are. For example, a month ago a brother, while having fellowship with the Lord, may have touched the matter of humility under the enlightening of the Lord. That day when he came out from his fellowship with the Lord and went to contact people, the humility seen in him was his newness in life. However, one month has passed since then, and he has not learned anything new. It is the same humility every day. The humility he has this month is the same as the humility he had a month ago. Let me tell you, a month ago his humility was in newness of life, but today his humility is no longer in newness of life. To have newness in life, one must live daily in fellowship with the Lord. Only this kind of humility is in newness of life, as the manna that is new every day. Sometimes when you meet certain brothers and sisters, you feel that they are good and faultless, yet they look so old. It is true that they are humble, but they are old, and there is no freshness in them. This is because they do not live in life.

It is the same way with our service. Whenever we live in spirit, our service will be fresh. It is carried out not according to old rules or old practices.

Life and Spirit Being One

Now we come to chapter eight. The utterance in this chapter is very interesting because it joins the Spirit and life together. Verse 2 says "the Spirit of life." The Chinese Union Version renders this term into "the Spirit who gives life," as if life and the Spirit are two entities. Actually it is not so. Life belongs to this Spirit, and this Spirit is a Spirit of life; the two are one. Life is the Spirit, and the Spirit is life.

Prior to chapter five, the book of Romans tells us that Christ is our Redeemer; in other words, Christ is our redemption. Then in the last half of chapter five it shows us that this Christ who became our redemption is our life. Now in chapter eight it shows us this life is the Spirit. Therefore, this book still follows the basic thought of the four Gospels. This Christ who came to be our redemption is our life, and in the end this life is the Spirit. This can be proven when we read on from 8:2. Verses 9 to 11 clearly show us that this Spirit who dwells in us is Christ Himself. Therefore, after all, like the Gospel of John, the book of Romans speaks about the story of the Spirit entering into man's spirit. I say again, this is the essence, the life, the soul, of Romans. Ultimately, Romans shows us that the Christ on the cross has become the Christ in us, that the objective Christ has become the subjective Christ, and that the Christ who accomplished redemption and who became our Savior has come into us as the Spirit of life.

Two Spirits Being Mingled to Become One Spirit

As we read on, we see in verse 16 that this Spirit is within us and is witnessing with our spirit. This Spirit, who is Christ Himself, is dwelling in us. Eventually, this Spirit is mingled with our spirit as one.

Needing to Walk according to the Spirit

From this point on, the book of Romans begins to show us that today, as those who have received grace, we do not need to do so many other things. It is not necessary for you to love others, to do good deeds, to reform your character, to improve your behavior, or to struggle and strive. None of these are necessary. Now the only thing that is necessary is to walk according to the spirit, as mentioned in 8:4-5. It is sufficient if you would just walk closely according to the spirit. Now you need to care for the spirit and be mindful of the spirit. In other words, you need to set your mind on the spirit. At the point when the book of Romans reaches its peak, it shows us that the Christ who accomplished redemption is this Spirit today, and this Spirit has come into your spirit and has become one with your spirit. This is the highest peak of

Romans. The book of Romans does not require you to improve your behavior or to do good deeds. You do not need to do anything else except to be responsible to this Spirit by setting your mind on Him and walking according to Him; this is sufficient.

The Spirit Interceding for Us

Then verse 26 of chapter eight mentions another point: The Spirit is doing a particular thing in us, that is, interceding for us. What is intercession? It is the groaning of the Holy Spirit to express God's desire for us. What is God's desire concerning us? It is to make us the same as His Son. God's desire is that we would be conformed to the image of His Son, and it is for this that the Spirit who dwells in our spirit is groaning. We may use an illustration here. A mother may desire that her son go to college; this is the mother's desire. When this mother sees that her son is not studying diligently, she groans. This groaning expresses the desire of the mother. The Spirit in us has a desire, and this desire is that we would be like the Son of God. However, we do not care for God's will, nor do we fit into His desire, so this indwelling Spirit groans continually. This groaning is a crying out of God's desire, and it is also a response to God's desire. This is Romans 8. As to the outward circumstances, they are the "all things" raised up by the mighty Spirit to help in the fulfillment of God's desire in us, and the Spirit causes these "all things" to work together for good to us. What is the good? The good refers to our being conformed to the image of God's Son.

The Spirit Being the Kernel,
the Essence, of Romans

Brothers and sisters, you need to see clearly that Romans is the first book of the Epistles and its kernel, its essence, is the spirit. Therefore, Romans is not a book on redemption, nor is it a book on justification. Instead, Romans is a book on the Spirit of life. It speaks altogether about the Spirit of life. In order to have the Spirit of life come into us, we need redemption and justification. However, redemption and justification are not the central thought of Romans. The central thought of Romans is that this Spirit comes into us to become our life, and we simply live according to this Spirit, walk according to this Spirit, care for this Spirit, and set our mind on this Spirit. This Spirit often groans in us according to the desire of God, expressing from deep within us a response to God's desire, which is that we would be completely conformed to the image of His Son. This is the essence of the book of Romans.

Chapter Three

THE SPIRIT IN ROMANS

(2)

Scripture Reading: Rom. 7:24-25; 8:1, 4-6; 12:2, 11; 14:17

THE SPIRIT OF LIFE
GIVING US SUBJECTIVE SALVATION

In the preceding chapter we saw that the Lord who accomplished redemption is the Spirit of life today. He died on the cross to redeem us who were fallen, to quicken us who were dead, to restore us who were damaged, and to cleanse us who were defiled. In this way He accomplished redemption. This is shown in the section before Romans 5:10. From 5:10 on, the book turns from redemption to life, showing us that the redeeming Christ is the Spirit of life today. Formerly, on the cross He was doing the objective work of redemption outside of us. Today He is doing the subjective work of salvation in us. Therefore, Romans 5:10 may be considered the key to the entire book. This verse says that we were reconciled through the death of God's Son, that is, through His work of redemption on the cross, and that having been reconciled, much more we will be saved in His life. This being saved refers to the saving work that is being carried out today by the redeeming Lord who has come into us as the Spirit of life.

Redemption is objective; salvation is subjective. Redemption has already been accomplished; salvation is still in progress. Redemption is altogether a matter of position; salvation is totally a matter of experience. Formerly He was the Redeemer; today He is the Spirit of life.

The subjective salvation by the Spirit of life in us consists clearly of five steps: setting us free, sanctifying us, transform-ing us, conforming us to the image of God's Son, and blending us together to produce the Body of Christ.

As those who have been redeemed by Christ, we were for-given of our sins, we are no longer under condemnation, and we are saved. From now on, however, we still need to have the various experiences of salvation in life. We still need the Spirit of life in us to daily set us free from sin. Of course, sin involves the flesh and the world. Therefore, to be freed from sin is to be released from the flesh and from the world that we may be delivered out of all the things that contradict and oppose God. Furthermore, the Spirit of life sanctifies us. This is not only an objective, positional sanctification but even more a dispositional sanctification. Once we are sanctified, we are transformed. This life saturates, permeates, and trans-forms us. As a result, we are sanctified.

Suppose you have a glass of water and a glass of orange juice. If you pour the orange juice slowly into the water, then the water will gradually turn yellow, and eventually it is "yel-lowed." Originally, we were like a glass of water, and the Lord as the Spirit is like the orange juice. The more the Spirit fills us, saturates us, and permeates us, the more He sanctifies us. This sanctification is not merely carried out by His hand but by His own divine nature. This is salvation in life.

Today when those who are in Christianity talk about sanc-tification and holiness, they only tell people, "You should not be defiled by sin, nor should you lose your temper. Otherwise, you become unholy. You have to be gentle, proper, and well-behaved, and then you are considered holy." This is what today's Christianity teaches about holiness. Actually this is not the holiness taught in the Bible. When the Bible speaks about holiness, the emphasis is not on our being cleansed but on our being made holy. In order to make us holy, God does not simply separate us by using a certain method. Rather, He saturates and transforms us completely with Himself.

After we have been set free and sanctified, we are trans-formed. The "water" has become "yellow." This is not the result of adding color on the outside but the issue of a change from within. Furthermore, there is conformation, that is, being conformed to the image of God's Son. Moreover, He wants to blend us together. This is because His desire is not only to gain many precious souls or many pieces of living stones. His desire is to have a building, a Body. Therefore, it is not enough that we are transformed and conformed to His image. He also wants to build us together.

The ultimate manifestation as seen at the end of the Scriptures is not a group of separate pieces of precious stones but a holy city, New Jerusalem. It is not enough for us just to be spiritual; we need to be spiritual and also built up together. Therefore, we need to be saved from being independent. This also needs the life within us to do a saving work. The life we have is the life of the Body; the more this life grows in us, the more we will grow together as one. We are not only being coordinated and built together, but we are also growing together into one entity.

Our physical life is a body life, not a member life. If the hand is detached from the body, the hand loses its life. It is the same with the spiritual life. The salvation carried out by this life eventually will save us from being independent so that we may become one Body. Therefore, in chapter twelve, the final section of Romans, we see the appearing of the one Body.

THE KEY TO OUR EXPERIENCING
THE SALVATION OF LIFE BEING OUR MIND

Now we want to focus on chapter eight. How do we experience the salvation of life mentioned above? This matter is absolutely related to our knowledge of the spirit. In order to experience the salvation in life, you need to experience Christ as the Spirit of life. If you want to experience Him as the Spirit of life, you must know your spirit and learn to discern the spirit from the soul. I absolutely believe that now you can easily discern and know that which is of the spirit and that which is of the soul. Besides this, in order to experience Christ as the Spirit of life, we also need to know our mind. We should not take the matter of the mind lightly. Many difficulties arise simply because we do not know how to use our mind, and we use it wrongly.

We know that even in receiving the salvation of the Lord we need to cooperate with Him. This may be illustrated by eating. After someone has prepared a meal for you, you still must cooperate by eating. If you do not eat or drink, you cannot receive the food into you. This illustration is very clear. Therefore, although the Lord wants to afford us the salvation of life, He needs our cooperation. If our cooperation is lacking, salvation cannot be realized.

However, the primary key to our cooperation with the Lord is actually not in the spirit but in the mind. This is because until now the real problem of the fallen man is in his mind and not in his spirit. If you know how to control, regulate, and employ the mind, then you are a proper person. Very often our difficulties arise from our mind.

Concerning this matter, I have to come back and say that in the church we also need to minister the word a great deal because the word can render help to the mind. The problems of people today are in their mind, so they need the word to correct, to help, to open, to enlighten, and to instruct them in their mind. The word is mainly related to the mind.

For a person to be saved, the most important thing is not for his spirit to be moved but for his mind to be opened. If he would open his mind, then it will be easy for his spirit to be moved. Second Corinthians 4 says that "if our gospel is veiled, it is veiled in those who are perishing, in whom the god of this age has blinded the thoughts of the unbelievers" (vv. 3-4a). When you preach one or two messages, you destroy Satan's binding power and remove his covering on people. Thus, you will cause people's minds to be opened to God, and the light of God will be able to shine into their spirit through their mind. Hence, the key to our salvation is in our mind, and the key to the exercise of our spirit is also in our mind. If we want to know how to exercise our spirit, we must know how to use our mind.

The Independent Mind Issuing in Death

The book of Romans shows us that the Christian's mind consists of three phases, three stages. In chapter seven, the mind may be considered our own mind, an independent mind.

Ordinarily when we say we struggle and strive by ourselves, in reality, it simply means that our mind intends to act independently. We feel that we must please God, so we use our mind to focus on how to behave well, how to do good works, and how to keep God's commandments.

Romans 7 does not say that man is doing bad things by his mind. Instead, it tells us that man is trying to do good and to keep the law of God by his mind. However, his mind is an independent mind. Today's Christians do not try to keep God's law as Paul did when he was under the law, but they still try to use their mind to do good things. After hearing a message with our mind, we may feel that it is a good message and we are deeply moved, so we consider how to work it out. This is an independent mind. An independent mind does not necessarily want to sin. On the contrary, very often it intends to do good in order to please God.

However, when the mind is independent, whether in doing bad things or in doing good things, the principle is the same: it is disconnected from the spirit. The Spirit of life is in your spirit, and when you are disconnected from your spirit, you are independent of the Lord, and when you are independent of the Lord, where are you then? Please remember that the experience in Romans 7 is the experience of the tree of the knowledge of good and evil. Once you are independent of the Lord, this will result in your falling into the tree of knowledge. Every time you try to do good or try to be spiritual by exercising your mind, that means you are eating of the tree of knowledge once again and the result is death. You need to know that not only your going to movies or losing your temper will result in death, but even when you, by your mind, try to work out the message which you heard or the Bible passage with which you were touched, it will also result in death. This is because both are of the tree of knowledge. One is the death brought in by the evil of the tree of the knowledge of good and evil, and the other is the death brought in by the good of the tree of the knowledge of good and evil. Both issue in death.

Romans 7 is the tree of the knowledge of good and evil, just as Romans 8 is the tree of life. The man in chapter eight is simply enjoying the tree of life, while the man in chapter seven is eating the fruit of the tree of the knowledge of good and evil every day, although here he eats only the good fruit and not the bad fruit. Whether it is the good fruit or the bad fruit, both lead to his death. Therefore, he says, "Wretched man that I am! Who will deliver me from the body of this death?" (v. 24). He is so desirous to keep the law, yet the result is death. This is the death that comes from eating the fruit of the tree of knowledge. This is the result of the mind being independent. You have an independent mind when your mind is not set on the spirit and is detached from the spirit.

The Mind Being Dependent on the Spirit to Experience Salvation

Thank the Lord, in Romans 8 the mind enters into another stage. It is no longer an independent mind but rather a trusting mind, a dependent mind. A person who has such a mind constantly sets his mind on the spirit and no longer strives by himself. Even when he is very touched after hearing a good message or reading an excellent portion of the Word, his mind is not set on the message. Rather, his mind is set on the spirit. His mind is not an independent mind but a dependent mind, a mind that trusts absolutely in the spirit. At this time his mind is completely joined to the spirit. In other words, he is in union with the spirit, and his soul is completely dependent on the spirit.

This is very different from the story of man's fall. In the fall of man, his soul became independent of his spirit. Putting the spirit aside, the soul acts and chooses on its own. Romans 8 is a real salvation because the soul is no longer independent but rather is dependent, relying, and set on the spirit.

Dear brothers and sisters, this is the secret to our experiencing the Lord Jesus as the Spirit of life and His subjective salvation in life. We need to set our mind on the spirit, continually be joined with the spirit as one, and never be detached from the spirit.

Many Christians have the concept that our prayer is to receive power from the Lord so that the Lord's power can help us to overcome. This concept is wrong. Prayer is not for you to ask the Lord to give you His power objectively. Rather, prayer is for your independent mind to become a dependent mind. The more you pray, the more your mind is turned back; hence, it becomes less an independent mind and more a dependent mind. Our prayer is the calling back of the mind. The more you pray, the more your mind, which represents you, is turned and set on the spirit. Once your mind is set on the spirit, it is like an electric appliance being plugged into the electrical socket and being connected to the source of electricity. Once you are "connected to the source of electricity," salvation comes. The Spirit within you begins to carry out the saving work for you to be set free, sanctified, transformed, conformed, and blended. Therefore, the key to experiencing the subjective salvation of the Lord as the Spirit of life within us is to set our mind on the spirit.

It is a pity that throughout the years none of the many who expounded the book of Romans and who spoke about the pathway to spirituality were able to point out this matter. We ourselves also could not point this out ten or twenty years ago. Today, however, we have seen clearly that the key to our cooperating with the Lord is to learn to set our mind on the spirit continually. As an illustration, certain brothers are true experts at operating tape recorders. If I were to operate them, I might act foolishly. I might try to turn the reels by hand, but that would be a human work. I might try to clean them and make them look very nice, but regardless of how nice they would look, they still would not turn. Yet these brothers, being very smart, simply put the plugs in the sockets, and the machines begin to operate. It does not matter if the machines are a little dirty; as long as they are connected to the electricity, they work. Brothers and sisters, it is the same way with us today. Regardless of how much you try to make yourself proper and well-behaved, even to the extent of not saying one wrong word, this may be due only to your inborn nature or your good upbringing. Anyone who is experienced can immediately tell that you are not connected to the Lord inwardly. Whether or not you are connected with the Lord does not depend on your broad-mindedness or magnanimity. Rather, it depends on where your mind is set. If it is set on the spirit, that is sufficient.

In these years in the United States, especially in Los Angeles, I pointed out this matter strongly. The light shone so intensely that many brothers and sisters were delivered in this matter. On the objective side, the messages we released in the recent years deal with how God wants Christ to be our life and the church to be the expression of Christ. On the subjective side, they first deal with the exercise of our spirit, and second, with setting our mind on the spirit. Countless brothers and sisters were blessed and set free in these two points.

Our co-workers must pay sufficient attention to this matter and have sufficient experience of it, and then you should go and help the brothers and sisters to know it in a real way. We have already enjoyed objective redemption, but today we still need to experience subjective salvation, that is, to experience Christ as our life. By what way? In brief, it is by setting the mind continually on the spirit. You simply must set your mind continually on your spirit, then the two are connected, and once the connection is made, salvation is here. Therefore, setting the mind on the spirit is the way for us to cooperate with the Lord's salvation.

Today the Lord has already prepared everything for us, and He is also in our spirit. All that is required is our cooperation, which is to set our mind on our spirit. Praise and thank the Lord, it is enough if you practice this. You do not need to strive or to exert effort. It is enough just to set your mind on your spirit. Henceforth, you simply walk according to the spirit.

The Mind Needing to Be Renewed and Transformed

The mind that is set on the spirit needs to be renewed and transformed because it is old. Therefore, we need to listen to messages and read the Bible, because listening to messages and reading the Scriptures can transform our mind. For example, someone may have a concept that to be personally spiritual is sufficient. He has fellowship with the Lord, and he also sets his mind on the spirit, but he thinks that it is all right as long as he pursues to be spiritual individually. This concept limits the Spirit's operation. Therefore, he needs to continue listening to messages and reading the Scriptures without subjectivity, so that the mind may be renewed. In this way he gradually feels that his previous concept was wrong because what God wants is not individual spirituality but the Body. When there is such a turn in his thinking, this is called renewing. Once this renewing occurs, the Spirit within is able to operate further. Therefore, there is the need for the word, both of the messages and the Scriptures, to change our mind, our concept.

When I went to Shanghai for the first time in 1933, I noticed that the sisters dared not to open their mouth in the meetings, because at that time there was the concept that 1 Corinthians 14 charges the sisters to be silent in the meetings. One day Brother Nee came to fellowship with me. He said that he had a feeling that when the sisters do not pray in the meetings, it is as if the church is paralyzed. But since 1 Corinthians 14 says that the sisters should be silent, he did not know what to do. Later he fellowshipped with some elderly co-workers and had a breakthrough in this matter. From then on the sisters began to break their silence and pray in the meetings.

In 1963 in Los Angeles, one day after the meeting a brother who was meeting somewhere else sought me out specially to argue. He said. "Brother Lee, your group claims that your meetings are altogether according to the Bible, but I feel that you are hardly according to the Bible. You ask the sisters to pray vocally, but the Scripture clearly says the sisters should be silent." I said, "Brother, do the sisters sing hymns in your meetings?" He said, "They do." Then I said, "That means your sisters are not silent either. Therefore, you are also acting contrary to the Bible. Brother, it is not simple to know the Scriptures. If you study 1 Corinthians 14 carefully, you will see that the sisters' being silent means that they should not teach in the meetings as teachers. How can it be God's intention that the sisters should not make any sound, not even sounds of praise, in the meetings!"

By this you can see that this is a matter of concept. If our concept is not turned around, then it is hard for the Lord's Spirit to operate without hindrance. Therefore, we have to get rid of not only our old concepts and old views concerning the world, but we also have to abandon our opinions concerning spiritual matters. We need to turn and study more of the Lord's words in the Bible so that our mind may be renewed and transformed.

Now you can see the three stages of the mind. The first stage is an independent mind, the second stage is a dependent mind, and the third stage is a transformed mind. After these three stages, our mind becomes a spiritual mind, which is fit for the Lord's use.

THE SPIRIT NEEDING TO BE BURNING AND REJOICING

Finally, your spirit needs to be burning and hot. The mind should be dependent and renewed, and the spirit should be burning. When your spirit is burning, the Holy Spirit is rejoicing. The joy in the Holy Spirit comes from this. At this point, there is the service, and there is also the living. This is the essence, the marrow, of Romans.

Brothers and sisters, I have outlined only the crucial points, hoping that you will dig into these points yourselves. You have to speak these matters and help the brothers and sisters know that the book of Romans shows us a redeeming Christ and that this redeeming Christ became the Spirit of life to carry out the subjective salvation in us. This subjective salvation includes five major steps: setting free, sanctification, transformation, conformation, and blending for building. Furthermore, this Spirit of life dwells in our spirit, and we need to cooperate with Him. First, our mind, which represents us, must be set on the spirit. Second, our mind must be renewed by the Lord's word. In this way we do not have our own view, nor will we be influenced by others. Instead, we do everything according to the Word; whatever the Word says, that is what we do. Praise and thank the Lord, this is sufficient. The result of this is that we are burning in spirit. I dare to guarantee you that your spirit within will be burning. If the brothers are all in this, and you also help the saints in various localities to be in this way, then the churches will be burning. This will be a true revival.

The burning in Romans 12:11 and the joy in 14:17 are the normal living and service of a Christian. Rejoicing is our living, and burning is our service. This is the story in the spirit. Consequently, the one Body is manifested.

This is not to say that all Christians are like this. Even in the age of the apostles, not every Christian took the way of the apostles. If you read Philippians, clearly there were some who did not take the way of the apostles and yet they also preached Christ. Today you cannot possibly ask all Christians to take the same way you are taking. This is not a responsibility we can bear. The responsibility we can bear is to know that this redeeming Christ who became the Spirit of life lives in our spirit to carry out His subjective salvation of life in us, and that we should cooperate with Him by always setting our mind on the spirit and letting His word illuminate our mind, thereby transforming it. Thus, He can get through and spread in us, and our spirit becomes burning while the Holy Spirit also is rejoicing. In this way we are blended and coordinated with a group of brothers and sisters. Toward those who are weaker and those who are ignorant, we just sympathize with them, love them, and try our best to care for them without any discrimination. However, with those who know this way we have to be blended and coordinated in love to serve as one Body, and at the same time, with all the brothers and sisters we would widely preach the gospel for the building up of the church of God. This is the way that is pleasing to God, and this is the way we want to take today.

CHAPTER FOUR

THE SPIRIT IN FIRST CORINTHIANS

GOD MAKING CHRIST EVERYTHING TO US

In 1 Corinthians chapter one the apostle Paul tells us that God's intention is to give Christ to us as our everything instead of giving us so many other things. There is a background to the apostle's speaking. At that time, like the Pentecostals today, the believers in Corinth emphasized gifts and especially stressed speaking in tongues. Therefore, Paul wrote this Epistle to tell them that what God gives us is not tongues, nor gifts, nor signs, nor wonders. Rather, what God gives us is Christ, who is our portion. God has called us not into tongues, signs, or wonders but into the fellowship of His Son, Christ. The Jews require signs and the Greeks seek wisdom, but God gives us Christ to be our wisdom and our power. God also puts us in Christ that Christ may become wisdom to us. This wisdom includes righteousness, sanctification, and redemption, which refers to the transfiguration of our body in the future. None of these matters are objective; instead, they are all Christ Himself. Christ Himself has become our righteousness, our sanctification, and our redemption. This means that God is working Christ into us for our participation.

The hardest thing in reading the Scriptures is that it is not easy to stay away from the non-essential items. When a person comes to read the Scriptures, he is frequently hindered by the superficial things and is thus unable to see the inner things. Generally, when Christians read 1 Corinthians, they say that chapter one speaks about not being divisive. Actually, this is not the focus of that chapter. That chapter is focused on Christ. Christ is our portion, and we have been called to enjoy Him. But when someone reads 1 Corinthians 1, he is easily blinded by the words concerning not being divisive; he sees division but not Christ. This may be compared to the way we look at a person; we are easily blinded by the outward appearance and are not able to see what is in his heart. Likewise, the Bible has its outward appearance, and it has also its spirit, its core. When we come to read the Scriptures, it is very easy for us to be hindered by the appearance.

First Corinthians does not speak about anything other than Christ. Chapter one tells us that the Jewish religionists require signs, while the Greek philosophers seek wisdom. But what God gives us is neither philosophy, nor religion, nor miraculous power, nor knowledge, nor wisdom; what God gives us is Christ Himself. Christ is the power for signs and wonders, and Christ is the highest wisdom. It is of God that we are in Christ. It is God who has put us in Christ so that Christ may become our wisdom, our method, and our way, firstly as our righteousness, secondly as our sanctification, and thirdly as our redemption. Christ becomes everything to us from the inside to the outside, and we are thus completely mingled with Him. This is the first chapter of 1 Corinthians.

THE EXPERIENCE OF CHRIST BEING IN OUR SPIRIT

From chapter two on, 1 Corinthians begins to speak about how we can experience this Christ. In order to experience this Christ, first we must realize that this Christ is Spirit and He is also in the Spirit. Second, we must also know that as the Spirit He dwells in our spirit, and if we want to experience and enjoy Him, we must come back to our spirit. We must know how to return to our spirit and how to use our spirit. With these few sentences I have covered 1 Corinthians chapters two through sixteen.

However, I am afraid that after reading the book of 1 Corinthians five or six times, we may still not have such a realization. On the contrary, we can readily see that chapter five deals with excommunication, chapter six deals with lawsuits among brothers, chapter seven deals with the matter of marriage, chapter eight deals with the prohibition against eating the things sacrificed to idols, chapter twelve deals with speaking in tongues, chapter thirteen deals with love, chapter fourteen deals with the various gifts, and chapter fifteen deals with the matter of resurrection. But I want to tell you, brothers and sisters, that these are still the superficial matters. You need to go beyond these superficial things to see the intrinsic matters. Simply speaking, intrinsically, this book shows us that today the Christ whom God has given to us for our enjoyment is not only in the Spirit but also is the Spirit. Furthermore, as the Spirit He is in our spirit, and if we truly want to have fellowship with Him, to enjoy Him, and to participate in Him, then we must come back to our spirit to contact Him as the Spirit. This is what chapter two to chapter sixteen speaks about.

You may ask what my basis for saying this is. If you read chapter two, you will find the spirit. Verse 14 in chapter two says, "But a soulish man [that is, one who lives according to the soul and in the soul] does not receive the things of the Spirit of God, for they are foolishness to him." May I ask you, what are the things of the Spirit of God? By reading the preceding verses you will know that they refer to the very Christ Himself. In verse 2 the apostle says, "I did not determine to know anything among you except Jesus Christ, and this One crucified." Therefore, the things of the Spirit of God refer to Christ.

Furthermore, verses 9 and 10 say, "'Things which eye has not seen and ear has not heard and which have not come up in man's heart; things which God has prepared for those who love Him.' But to us God has revealed them through the Spirit." Again, I would like to ask you, brothers and sisters, what are the things which God has prepared for us? When I was a child, I heard an old pastor telling me that what God prepared for us is heaven, a place which is so wonderful that it has not been seen by human eye or heard by human ear, nor has it ever come up in man's heart. But now I want to ask you, brothers and sisters, what do these verses really speak about? Oh, they tell us that God has prepared Christ as everything to us! This matter is incomprehensible to a soulish man.

Verses 14-15a say, "But a soulish man does not receive the things of the Spirit of God, for they are foolishness to him and he is not able to know them because they are discerned spiritually. But the spiritual man discerns all things." Here we see there are two kinds of men: the soulish man who lives according to the soul and the spiritual man who lives according to the spirit. Only those who live in spirit can know Christ, apprehend Christ, and enjoy Christ in spirit.

I want to take this opportunity to speak a word to the brothers who minister the word. I hope that from now on when you minister the word, you will elaborate on these matters. God has given Christ to us as our portion. Today if we want to experience this Christ and enter into His fellowship, we must realize that this is altogether a story in the spirit. Therefore, we all must be in the spirit and not in the soul. This passage says clearly that there are two kinds of men: the soulish man and the spiritual man. The spirit is a faculty created for us by God that we may have contact and communication with Him, and it is also His vessel to contain Himself, while the soul is man himself. We must point these matters out clearly to the brothers and sisters. Do not think that speaking about these matters once or twice is sufficient. Some people cannot grasp them even after hearing them a hundred times.

I can share a testimony with you. Two or three months after I was saved, I began to read some articles concerning the distinction between the spirit and the soul. I continued to read about this matter, and when I went to Shanghai, I also listened to many messages concerning this matter, but I simply could not understand it. Moreover, I heard some brothers say that a person cannot be spiritual unless he knows how to discern the spirit. When I went home after hearing that word, I could neither sleep nor eat well because I did not know how to discern the spirit. But gradually after a few more times of listening to the messages about this matter, one day suddenly it became clear to me within. Therefore, you should not be afraid of repeating the same message, thinking that there is no need to repeat a message after it has been given. This feeling may not be accurate. It is not a matter of whether or not to repeat, but a matter of whether or not the speaker is living. If you are living, your speaking will also be living.

After 1 Corinthians chapter one mentions that Christ is our portion, chapter two immediately touches the matter of the spirit. Why? It is because Christ being our portion is basically a story of the spirit. This matter is not physical, philosophical, religious, or doctrinal. Rather, it is altogether a matter in the spirit. If you are not in the spirit but instead live in the soul, you are one whose eyes are covered. Therefore, when it speaks about how to experience Christ, chapter two immediately mentions the spirit. Paul speaks about Christ in chapter two in a marvelous way. In essence he says, "When I came to you, I only knew to speak Christ, and this Christ is what God has prepared for us, which is beyond what we can think and which requires the Spirit to explain to us." Recall what the Lord Jesus said: "No one fully knows the Son except the Father" (Matt. 11:27). Then in Matthew 16, after Peter said to the Lord, "You are the Christ, the Son of the living God," the Lord immediately said, "Blessed are you, Simon Barjona, because flesh and blood has not revealed this to you, but My Father who is in the heavens" (vv. 16-17). Therefore, unless the Spirit of the Father reveals the Lord Jesus to us, and unless the Spirit of the Father removes the veil from our eyes and shows Christ to us in our spirit, we will not be able to know Him. In order to know and experience this Christ, we must learn to not live in the soul but to live in the spirit. When you are in the spirit, you touch Him. You should not use your eyes to see Him, nor use your ears to hear Him, nor use your heart to think about Him; rather, you should use your spirit to touch Him. Therefore, you must be a person in spirit.

THE INDWELLING SPIRIT BEING CHRIST HIMSELF

Now we come to 1 Corinthians chapter three. Many expositors acknowledge that this chapter speaks most clearly of the Spirit being the indwelling Spirit. Verse 16 says, "Do you not know that you are the temple of God, and that the Spirit of God dwells in you?" Here a question arises: Who is this indwelling Spirit? To get the answer we need to skip over to 6:17, which says, "He who is joined to the Lord is one spirit." By reading 3:16 and 6:17 together you will naturally understand that the indwelling Spirit is the Lord Himself. If the indwelling Spirit were not the Lord Himself, how could we be joined to the Lord as one spirit? Hence, these two verses show us that this indwelling Spirit is just the Lord Himself.

First Corinthians 6:17 is a great verse in the Scriptures. Some consider that "God so loved the world that He gave His only begotten Son" is the greatest verse in the Bible, but I think it is not as great as 1 Corinthians 6:17. Please consider: what can be greater than the fact that you can be joined to the Lord as one spirit? This verse tells us two great matters: first, the Lord Himself is the Spirit, and second, the Lord and we are joined as one spirit. This being the case, this union must have transpired in our spirit. Otherwise, how could He be joined to us as one spirit? Therefore, this verse shows us that this Christ is the indwelling Spirit and that He as the indwelling Spirit surely must be in our spirit. For this reason the apostle Paul went on to say that if we want to know and experience this Christ, we need to be those who are in spirit. We must be spiritual men instead of soulish men.

At this point, brothers and sisters, I believe that the light is sufficiently clear to you. Beginning from chapter two, this Epistle is not dealing with division, nor with excommunication due to fornication, nor with lawsuits among brothers, nor with the matter of marriage. Instead, it is speaking about Christ, the God-given portion, who is the indwelling Spirit and who lives now in our spirit. In order to participate in Him, have fellowship with Him, experience Him, and enjoy Him, we need to turn to our spirit. The reason you have division is that you are not in the spirit. You live in the flesh, and therefore you are liable to commit fornication and to bring a lawsuit against a brother.

CHRIST AS THE LAND OF CANAAN
AND AS THE BLESSING IN THE HOLY OF HOLIES

Here I would like to point out another matter. Chapter three and chapter six of 1 Corinthians also mention the fact that we are the temple. There are clearly three parts to the temple. One part is the outer court, another part is the Holy Place, and yet another part is the Holy of Holies. Please remember, the fleshly man lives in the outer court, the soulish man lives in the Holy Place, and the spiritual man lives in the Holy of Holies. In other words, our spirit is our Holy of Holies. The brother in Corinth who committed such a grave sin of fornication was a fleshly man. In fact, he was not only fleshly but fleshy. The flesh has different degrees of seriousness. Being divisive is of a less serious nature, and one who is divisive is *fleshly;* whereas, committing fornication is of a more serious nature, and one who commits fornication is *fleshy.* At any rate, in 1 Corinthians we see three kinds of men: the fleshy and fleshly man, the soulish man, and the spiritual man. If you live in the flesh, you are in the outer court; if you live in the soul, you are in the Holy Place; and if you live in the spirit, you are in the Holy of Holies.

If you read 1 Corinthians carefully, you will be able to see another matter, that is, when the apostle wrote the Epistle, he took the Israelites' exodus from Egypt and their entrance into Canaan as a background. In 5:7 he said that our Passover, Christ, had been sacrificed. And in 10:1-4 he said that "all our fathers were under the cloud, and all passed through the sea; and all were baptized unto Moses in the cloud and in the sea; and all ate the same spiritual food, and all drank the same spiritual drink; for they drank of a spiritual rock which followed them." This obviously refers to the situation of the children of Israel in the wilderness. Then 10:11 says that the things that happened to the children of Israel were written for our admonition. This tells us that today we are in the wilderness. In chapter five we already passed through the Passover and are no longer in Egypt, and in chapter nine we are in the wilderness. Therefore, it tells us there that we should endeavor to go forward. Where are we going? We are going to Canaan. Then where is today's Canaan? This Canaan is the Christ in our spirit.

In the church in Corinth there were divisions and lawsuits among brothers. May I ask you, where were the believers who were in that kind of condition? On the one hand, they were in the outer court, and on the other hand, they were in Egypt. Furthermore, there were some who were daily involved with the so-called spiritual gifts. Where were these ones? They were in the soul. They lingered in the Holy Place and remained in the wilderness. Therefore, Paul told them not to wander in the wilderness any longer. The end of chapter nine says explicitly that we all are in a race. We must not stay where we are; rather, we must run and go forward.

The children of Israel in the wilderness were running on a racecourse. Today we are also running on a racecourse. Therefore, we should not linger here but go forward and run until we enter Canaan. We should no longer stay here playing with such gifts as speaking in tongues. God's goal is not speaking in tongues or any other gifts but Christ. Only Christ is our Canaan. You should not remain in the flesh to dispute with one another, nor should you remain in the soul to pay attention exclusively to the gifts. You need to turn from the flesh to the soul, and then from the soul to the spirit. You need to go from the outer court into the Holy Place, and then from the Holy Place into the Holy of Holies. You need to go from Egypt to the wilderness, and then from the wilderness to Canaan.

Paul wrote the book of 1 Corinthians with two backgrounds. The first background is the Israelites' exodus from Egypt, going through the wilderness, and entering into Canaan. The other background is the temple. Paul clearly told the believers in Corinth that they were the temple. He also said that they had already kept the Passover and had left Egypt, and now they were running in the wilderness. Therefore, he told them to be careful, because if they did not run well, they would fall dead in the wilderness. This means that they would fall dead in the soul and would not be able to enter the spirit to enjoy Christ. Therefore, they needed to go forward, not only overcoming the flesh but also overcoming the soul, and not only being delivered from the flesh but also being delivered from the soul. Not only should they refrain from remaining in the flesh, but they should also avoid remaining in the soul. Where then should they go? They have to go to the spirit to meet Christ there, because Christ is the Canaan which God has prepared for us today.

This matter is neglected by many Christians today. Many Christians do not see that 1 Corinthians presents Christ as our Canaan and as the blessing in the Holy of Holies, and it also reveals that our spirit is the Holy of Holies as well as the good land of Canaan. Today we should not live in our flesh or in our soul but in our spirit. Once we live in our spirit, we touch Christ in our spirit as our Canaan in reality. At such a time, we are spiritual men. Although we still have the flesh, we do not live according to the flesh; the flesh becomes insignificant to us. Although we are persons with a soul, it is in subjection to us, and we do not live according to it. Although we are persons who still have the flesh and the soul, we all live in the spirit and according to the spirit. Therefore, we and Christ are joined as one spirit. What people see in us is a condition of being one spirit. He is a Spirit, and He is also in our spirit. The two spirits, our spirit and He as the Spirit, are joined together. This is the living in the land of Canaan, and this is the living in the Holy of Holies.

THE SPIRIT IN 1 CORINTHIANS
BEING THE CHRIST IN SPIRIT

After pointing out some of these things to you, brothers and sisters, I believe that you surely must have seen something clearly. Now let me ask you again, what does 1 Corinthians chapters two to sixteen speak about? No doubt these chapters speak about some other matters, but those are simply "background drawings." It is a pity that today when people see these background drawings, they cling to them and cannot go on to see the central matters. Some can truly expound on the book of 1 Corinthians. They can present clearly and reasonably, by quoting Scripture verses, the matters of lawsuits, excommunication, and idol sacrifices. You cannot say that these things are wrong, but after reading through the entire commentary, you cannot find a passage telling you how to turn to the spirit to touch the pneumatic Christ. Brothers and sisters, I am afraid this is also what many of you know about 1 Corinthians. What I would like to tell you, however, is that God has called us into the fellowship of His Son to enjoy Him and that God has also put us in Christ, making Christ everything to us. Paul said that he did not know anything except this when he went out to work for the Lord. This is so mysterious, so rich, and so excellent that it has not been seen by man's eye or heard by man's ear. It all depends on the Spirit to reveal it in our spirit. If we want to see this, however, we must see the flesh and deny the soul; we must not live in the flesh or in the soul. When we live in the spirit, immediately we touch and perceive this. As a result, we are joined with this Spirit as one spirit. This means that we have not only left Egypt but also crossed the Jordan and entered Canaan. In Canaan we then enjoy the God-promised blessing, which is Christ. This means also that we have left the outer court, passed through the Holy Place, and entered the Holy of Holies, where we are enjoying Christ Himself in the glory of God. This is altogether a story in the spirit.

Dear brothers and sisters, please consider this. Is this what 1 Corinthians speaks about or not? First Corinthians shows us that filthy things such as fornication and idolatry are of the flesh and of the animal nature, and therefore we should not practice them. Furthermore, such things as being divisive, being contentious, being self-exalted, and being conceited, considering ourselves better than others, are fleshly, and therefore we should also not do them. Even the gifts, such as speaking in tongues, healing, and casting out demons, are wonderful, but they are still the things in the Holy Place; hence, we must not remain in them. We must lay these things down and touch Christ directly. We should be joined to Him as the Spirit to be one spirit and to experience Him in spirit. We must not be in the flesh or in the soul but in the spirit. In this way we can enter into Canaan. This is the spirit, the life, of 1 Corinthians. All the other things are peripheral things and background drawings showing us that when we are not living in the spirit, the first possibility is that we are fleshy, defiling ourselves. The second possibility is that we are fleshly—being jealous, divisive, proud, and despising others. And the third possibility is that we are in the Holy Place, touching the matters of the spirit but not the spirit itself. Therefore, the purpose of this book is that we enter into Canaan.

In the New Testament there are two books that tell us to enter into Canaan; one is 1 Corinthians and the other is Hebrews. These two books tell us to live in the spirit, and only these two books repeatedly speak about the discerning of the spirit from the soul. First Corinthians mentions the soulish man and the spiritual man, while Hebrews speaks about the dividing of soul and spirit. I hope that when the brothers come together to pray and to read the Word, they would also go in this direction. Just as in mining, one should not dig for worthless things but for diamonds and gold. And at the same time, you yourself must have some experiences in these matters. What the churches need the most these days is this kind of experience.

Finally, I say again, dear brothers and sisters, 1 Corinthians is altogether a book showing us that Christ is our everything. It is He Himself who is in us as our righteousness. When you live in the spirit and live by Him, He is your righteousness. When He is lived out of you, He becomes your righteousness. Not only so, when you live in and according to Him, He is then your holiness, and He sanctifies you. He does not sanctify you according to any method; rather, He sanctifies you with His nature. When you live by Him, He is your holiness and your righteousness. This means that in you there is nothing unlawful, nothing disorderly, and nothing which is not according to the truth. Whatever of Christ comes out of you is righteous and just and is all up to the standard. Speaking in a deeper way, it is all suited to God and fully compatible with God's nature. What you live out is just Christ Himself. Then one day, at His coming back, He Himself will come out of us through transformation. He is saturating us with Himself, and then at that time our whole body will enter into His glory. In this way He becomes our glory. That will be the redemption of our body. We will then be fully delivered out of the old creation, and we will be fully filled with Him within and without. This result is not accomplished by God using an objective method or an objective power. Rather, it is carried out by His transforming us subjectively with Himself as the element within us. Now we must turn to the spirit to touch the pneumatic Lord and to live by Him. We must fellowship with Him in the spirit all day long, and we must live daily in His fellowship, having communion with Him and enjoying Him as our blessing. If we live by Him daily, the result is that righteousness and sanctification will be lived out of us, and one day it will be seen in our body, which is the redemption of our body. This is the life of the book of 1 Corinthians.

Chapter Five

THE SPIRIT IN SECOND CORINTHIANS

Now we go on to 2 Corinthians, which experientially is altogether a continuation of 1 Corinthians. In 1 Corinthians the thought of the Holy Spirit is to show us that we need to enter into the spirit to enjoy the pneumatic Christ in the spirit and to experience Christ as the Spirit of life. First Corinthians shows us that we all are God's children, God's people, and we all are saved ones, saints. However, some of us are serving in the outer court, some are living in the Holy Place, and only a very small number have entered into the Holy of Holies to enjoy God's blessing—Christ Himself—in God's presence. Although all are saved ones, and all are Israelites, some are in Egypt, some are wandering in the wilderness, and some have entered into Canaan. Therefore, 1 Corinthians encourages us to be delivered not only from the flesh but also from the soul, to go on from the flesh, to pass through the soul, and to enter into the spirit and to live in the spirit. This is to enter into the Holy of Holies and enjoy the riches of Canaan in the spirit. This is the main flow of thought in 1 Corinthians. It seems that in this book there is a hidden flow, which is not so easy to be seen from the surface. If it were like a flow on the surface of the earth, it could be easily detected, but since it is a flow beneath the surface, unless you go under the earth, you will not be able to see it. Thank the Lord, we have more or less seen this.

BEING FORCED TO LIVE IN SPIRIT
DUE TO THE TEARING DOWN THROUGH SUFFERINGS

Following 1 Corinthians, 2 Corinthians goes on to speak altogether about how a person lives in the Holy of Holies, in the spirit. It also tells us that the reason this one can live in the Holy of Holies, in the spirit, is that he has been outwardly torn down, consumed, in many ways. In the entire New Testament, there is only one place which tells us that the Lord does not always answer our prayers in our times of suffering. Christianity usually teaches people that when they have some sufferings and have fallen into a difficult situation, they should simply tell the Lord, and the Lord will solve their problems and answer all their prayers. Nevertheless, 2 Corinthians 12 clearly shows us, with an illustration, that Paul had a thorn in his flesh which caused much suffering to him. He prayed three times to the Lord, asking the Lord to remove this thorn, to solve this problem for him, to save him from this suffering, but the Lord seemed to be saying, "I will not do it; I reject this prayer; I will not answer this prayer. I am letting the thorn remain there so that you can experience My all-sufficient grace. In order for you to experience that My overshadowing power is perfected in the weakness of man, I have to allow this thorn to make your weakness manifest. There must be a thorn to tear you down, to completely consume you, so that you will not come out of the Holy of Holies and turn back to yourself again. I leave this thorn in you to keep you in the Holy of Holies, to force you to live in the Holy of Holies. Therefore, I will not answer this prayer of yours."

Brothers and sisters, this thought is contrary to the teachings of Christianity. What you usually hear in Christianity is that if you have any problem, the Lord will rescue you; if you are in hardship, the Lord will visit you; no matter what disaster happens to you, the Lord will take care of it for you. However, in the sixty-six books of the Scriptures there is a portion which tells us that the Lord will not listen to this kind of prayer. Therefore, remember that in the sixty-six books of the Bible only this one portion tells us that God wants to tear us down. Verse 16 of chapter four says, "Though our outer man is decaying, yet our inner man is being renewed day by day."

Please remember that 2 Corinthians has a particular position in the Holy Word. Experientially, 2 Corinthians occupies an exceptionally high position, and we may even say that it is on the peak, because in this Epistle Paul had already entered into the Holy of Holies and truly remained in the Holy of Holies. How could he enter the Holy of Holies and remain there? It is because his outer man was consumed. A thorn which came by the permission of the Lord (it was not sent but permitted by the Lord) and which was Satan's messenger, consumed Paul, causing him to enter the Holy of Holies.

According to our condition, we surely need some circumstances, circumstances that are not smooth or good but adverse and rough, to force us into the spirit. Please remember, when we are at ease, it is easy to get out of the spirit. We need various adverse situations to force us into the Holy of Holies.

THE KIND OF PERSONS BEING ABLE TO REMAIN IN SPIRIT

Brothers and sisters, I would like you to know that 1 Corinthians shows us a picture: Here there is a temple with a group of people: Some are in the outer court, others are in the Holy Place, and still others are in the Holy of Holies. First Corinthians seems also to show us a map: Some people are in Egypt, others are wandering in the wilderness, and only a few have entered into Canaan. As to the individuals, some are living by the flesh, which is very low. Others are living by the soul, and a few are living by the spirit. The book of 1 Corinthians shows us such a picture to encourage us to enter into the spirit and to live by the spirit. Then 2 Corinthians shows us what kind of persons are those who live in the spirit, who live in the Holy of Holies, and who remain in Canaan.

Being Excessively Burdened, beyond Their Power, and Not Trusting in Themselves

There are several portions in 2 Corinthians that we must definitely read. For example, 1:8-9 says, "For we do not want you to be ignorant, brothers, of our affliction which befell us in Asia, that we were excessively burdened, beyond our power, so that we despaired even of living. Indeed we ourselves had the response of death in ourselves, that we should not base our confidence on ourselves but on God, who raises the dead."

What is the self mentioned here? The self refers not to the flesh but to the soul. *We should not base our confidence on ourselves* may also be rendered as *we should not trust in ourselves*. Not trusting in ourselves does not refer to not trusting in ourselves to transact business, to pursue education, or to seek pleasure. Rather, it refers to not trusting in ourselves to work for God or to serve God. To not trust in ourselves is to be in the Holy of Holies, while to trust in ourselves is to be in the Holy Place.

Other examples are 4:16 and 12:9; these expressions can only be found in the book of 2 Corinthians. This is because 2 Corinthians, as a continuation of 1 Corinthians, shows us what kind of persons are able to live in the Holy of Holies, that is, in the spirit. These persons are the ones who are excessively burdened, beyond their power, so that they despair even of living and judge themselves to be utterly helpless and who therefore no longer trust in themselves. Only such ones can live in the spirit.

Conducting Themselves in the World
in Singleness and Sincerity of God

Verse 12 of chapter one says, "For our boasting is this, the testimony of our conscience, that in singleness [or, simplicity] and sincerity of God, not in fleshly wisdom but in the grace of God, we have conducted ourselves in the world." Paul spoke these words out of a very deep experience. When we live in the soul, that is, by ourselves, we are neither single nor simple; rather, we have many ways. But when we are excessively burdened, beyond our power, and in desperation, having exhausted all our human ways, we then live according to the singleness, the simplicity, of God.

Please consider the case of Jacob. Jacob was a very capable person who had so many ways before the socket of his hip was touched and he was crippled. Every one of us is a little Jacob. We also have many ways before we have been dealt with by God to a great extent. We still try to escape and hide. We are not simple! Yet look at Jacob. After he crossed over the ford of the Jabbok, the socket of his hip was touched by God; at that point he became simple. He became a completely different person. Formerly he had so many ways, but after his hip was dislocated and he was crippled, he had no ways at all. He then began to live in the singleness, the simplicity, of God.

After singleness is sincerity. Non-singleness is disguised insincerity. Paul conducted himself in the world in the singleness and sincerity of God. He did not depend on human wisdom; that is, he did not depend on the soul. Rather, he depended on God's favor, God's grace.

This portion of the Word tells us that Paul was one who lived in the Holy of Holies. He had crossed the Jordan. While the Red Sea buried the Egyptian armies, it was the Jordan that buried the children of Israel. Hence, Paul was already buried in the Jordan, and his self was already cut off, sifted out, filtered out. He really knew what it was to have no confidence in himself, to not depend on human wisdom, and what it was to base his confidence on God, who raises the dead, and on the grace of God. Here we see a person who was not in the flesh or in the soul, not in Egypt or in the wilderness, not in the outer court or in the Holy Place, but who was altogether in the Holy of Holies, in Canaan, in the spirit, enjoying God Himself. He was not enjoying God's help or God's rescue but Christ Himself.

Experiencing the Spirit as the Anointing and as the Pledge

Now let us consider 1:20-22: "For as many promises of God as there are, in Him is the Yes; therefore also through Him is the Amen to God, for glory through us to God. But the One who firmly attaches us with you unto Christ and has anointed us is God, He who has also sealed us and given the Spirit in our hearts as a pledge." We often expound these verses in a shallow way, but Paul's words were very deep in meaning. It was not until this time that he experienced how God had anointed him and had given the Spirit in him as a pledge. It was in the depths, in the Holy of Holies, that he experienced God's anointing ointment and the Spirit as a pledge. At this point in time he was one who truly lived in the spirit.

Brothers and sisters, please bear with me for coming back

to speak about the Pentecostal practices and, in particular, speaking in tongues. Please consider: When you were involved with the so-called gifts and were speaking in tongues, did you have the sense of the anointing deep inside of you? Did you have the sense of enjoying the Spirit as a pledge? You could not have had such sensations because those were superficial experiences, and you therefore could not sense the anointing or the Spirit's pledging in your depths. This is not to say that these charismatic experiences are all false (of course, some of them are false). However, even if they were real experiences, they would still be outward and superficial. It is not until you have been forced by God into the spirit, utterly burdened beyond your power, that you can begin to experience the Holy Spirit not superficially but in your depths. Only then will you know what the anointing within is all about. You will also know that it is not only a matter of the working of the Spirit within but that fundamentally the Spirit Himself within you is the pledge. What you experience is the Spirit Himself and not merely the working, the moving, the power, or the gift of the Spirit.

Captives of Christ

Chapter two shows us that we are captives of Christ. A person who is a captive has lost everything. He has no more opinions or views. If I were your captive, what opinion would I still have? If I would completely hand myself over to the Lord, surrendering my body, my will, my feeling, and my all, then I would be a person who has been delivered from the soul. Today, however, we are still living in the soul and unwilling to surrender all, so how can we be captives? We stand on the same level with the Lord Jesus; we negotiate with Him and deal with Him as if doing business transactions. Sometimes we ask Him, "O Lord, I have given you so much, and what will You give me?" Other times we ask, "Lord, You have given this to me, so how much do you want from me?" It is as if we are asking, "How much does it cost?" The Lord's answer is, "I want you." Then you may say, "No, I cannot pay such a price, so let us forget about it!" This is the story of a man in the soul. If we truly have been captured by the Lord, we will have no ground to negotiate with Him. We have been defeated, we have surrendered unconditionally, and we have become captives. What kind of persons are those who live in the Holy of Holies? They are those who have been completely captured by Christ.

SECOND CORINTHIANS COVERING
THE DEEPEST EXPERIENCE OF THE SPIRIT

Now we may come to chapter three. People say that Romans 8 is a chapter concerning the Holy Spirit, but I would like to tell you that the speaking of Romans 8 concerning the Holy Spirit is shallow and introductory. The deepest and highest speaking concerning the Holy Spirit is in 2 Corinthians chapter three. No one knows how much deeper 2 Corinthians 3 is than Romans 8 in speaking concerning the Holy Spirit. Romans 8 shows us only that we must walk according to the Spirit and that the Spirit is in us praying and groaning for us. It tells us only this much, and what we understand is that we are children of God to be His heirs. But 2 Corinthians 3 shows us that the Spirit within us is the letter-writing Spirit, who writes Christ into us over and over again. This writing of letters is through the environment. Romans 8 is like an elementary school, while 2 Corinthians 3 is like a college. In Romans 8 the experience of the Spirit within us is at the initial stage, while in 2 Corinthians 3 it has reached the peak. The Spirit is not only writing in us but also doing a constituting work in us. He not only gives us gifts but also makes us ministers.

May I ask you, that day when Balaam's donkey was able to speak a human language, was it a gift or a ministry? No doubt, that was a gift. Let me ask another question; when you speak Chinese, is it a gift or in the principle of a ministry? Your speaking Chinese today is in the principle of a ministry. Why? It is because since your childhood the Chinese language has been constituted into you.

Let me give another example. A certain brother may have enjoyed wonderful fellowship with the Lord in the last two days, so he is very meek and humble. Please tell me: Is his being meek and humble a gift or a ministry? We all are clear that it is a gift. Perhaps after two days, when the inspiration is gone, his rough manner will reappear. But if Paul were here today, having been pierced by a thorn, pressed by burdens, and torn down by God, he would have been constituted by God to such an extent that even if you tried to make him lose his temper, he would not be able to do it. His meekness did not come from inspiration.

Therefore, 2 Corinthians does not deal with gifts at all. Rather, it deals altogether with the constituting work carried out by the Spirit in the depths of our being to write the meekness of Christ into us. It is not the inspiration of the outward power causing us to show some godliness, after which, when the inspiration is gone, our original form reappears. God's purpose is for us to go on to 2 Corinthians and not to remain in 1 Corinthians, to enter Canaan and not to remain in the wilderness, to live continually in the Holy of Holies and not to turn back to the Holy Place.

Second Corinthians 3 depicts a life that is altogether in the Holy of Holies. Here we see a person who is living continually in the Holy of Holies, being written upon by God and constituted by the Spirit. Therefore, we can see that the entire chapter is speaking about the Spirit—not the Spirit of inspiration but the Spirit who gives life, not the Spirit of gifts but the Spirit of ministry, not the Spirit for us to experience in an outward, superficial, and shallow way but the Spirit who is constituting us from within. These two are altogether different.

Second Corinthians 3:17 tells us that the Lord is the Spirit. This is a unique word in the entire Scriptures. Only this portion in the Bible says it in this way. Today's Christianity typically says that the Lord works through the Holy Spirit. I am not against this saying, because there is this kind of saying in the Bible, but this is shallow. You have to go further and see that today the Spirit in us who is constituting us and writing on us is the Lord Himself. Today even in Christianity if you say that the Lord Jesus is the Spirit, some people will oppose you. I have heard people opposing this, and more than one have argued with me. However, I did not argue much. I simply said, "Brothers, you are right. I also acknowledge the Trinity you talk about, but let me ask you: Second Corinthians 3 says that the Lord is the Spirit; who is the Lord here? Of course, He is the Lord Jesus. Then who is the Spirit? Can it be that the Spirit here is not the Holy Spirit? If you say that the Spirit here is not the Holy Spirit, then this means that besides the Holy Spirit there is another Spirit. This is truly a heresy! If the Lord Jesus is not the Spirit, then how many are living in you today? The Bible tells us that the Lord Jesus lives in you, and the Bible also says that the Holy Spirit lives in you. If the Lord Jesus is not the Spirit, then how many are living in you?"

When we say that the Father is the Son and the Son is the Spirit, this is not a doctrinal explanation. Rather, we are speaking altogether from experience. Isaiah 9:6 says that "a son is given to us" and that "His name will be called...Mighty God, Eternal Father." Clearly He is the Son, yet He is also the Father. Furthermore, 2 Corinthians 3:17 says that the Lord is the Spirit. On the one hand, the Bible says that the Son is the Father, and on the other hand, it says that the Lord is the Spirit. This is the mystery of the divine persons, which I can neither comprehend nor explain. This is why the saints in the early days had to find a way to express it by using the term *the Triune God*. The persons are three, yet they are still one God, not three Gods. The Spirit who dwells in us is this God, the Lord Himself. The Lord is the Spirit.

The wonderful thing is that 2 Corinthians 3:17 says, on the one hand, "The Lord is the Spirit," and on the other hand, "Where the Spirit of the Lord is, there is freedom." It says, "The Lord is the Spirit," and it also says, "The Spirit of the Lord"; how do you explain this? If you ask me, I also cannot explain it. This is the mystery of the Triune God. Moreover, John 1:1 says, "In the beginning was the Word, and the Word was with God." This clearly indicates that the Word and God are two. Yet it goes on to say, "And the Word was God"; this shows that the Word and God are one. This matter is difficult to explain doctrinally, but once we have a deeper experience of the Lord, we will touch the fact. To be sure, the person in your spirit is the Spirit. According to your shallow experience, you may feel that the Lord Jesus is in the heavens, while the Holy

Spirit is here on earth inspiring you. If you only feel that the Lord Jesus is in the heavens, while the Holy Spirit is moving within us, enabling us to know, apprehend, and believe in the Lord Jesus, this kind of experience is shallow. Forgive me for saying that although this is precious, it is shallow. When your experience deepens, and when you are truly mingled with the Spirit, then you will know that the Spirit who is in you and who has mingled with you is the very Lord Himself.

When I was young, I heard people say that in the entire Scriptures there is no prayer addressed to the Holy Spirit, and that we have to ask the Father to give us the Holy Spirit and ask the Lord to pour down the Holy Spirit. At that time I felt that this is right, and even today I still acknowledge that this truth has its place in the Scriptures. However, gradually, one day in my experience I realized that the Lord is the Spirit; therefore, when I talk to the Spirit, I talk to the Lord, and when I talk to the Lord, I talk to the Spirit. It is true that the Bible does not tell us to pray to the Holy Spirit but tells us to pray only to the Father. Yet when our realization deepens to a certain degree, we will feel that praying to the Spirit is exactly the same as praying to the Father, because the Lord is the Spirit.

What I have just said shows you that when our experience of the Lord is shallow, we always feel that the Lord is far away and that the Holy Spirit is only a means by which we can know and experience the Lord. Gradually, however, as our experience of the Lord deepens to a certain extent, we will feel that it is not so. Instead, we have the realization that the Spirit who is working in us is the very Lord, that the One who is in us and who causes us to know the Lord is the Lord Himself. Eventually, you will say the Lord is the Spirit. All this is to tell us that the experience in 2 Corinthians 3 is deep.

Second Corinthians 3 has a special place in the truth. It has three kinds of expressions concerning the persons of the Triune God. First it says, "The Lord is the Spirit"; then it says, "The Spirit of the Lord"; and then in verse 18 it says, "The Lord Spirit," which is similar to saying "the Lord Jesus" or "the Father God." Just as "the Father God" denotes that the Father and God are one, so "the Lord Spirit" also denotes that the Lord and the Spirit are one. We seldom say, "Lord Spirit," but we do say, "Lord God." From now on we also have to learn to say, "Lord Spirit." Today it is the Lord Spirit who is working in us because it is the Lord Spirit who is transforming us and who is writing in us. As your experience of the Lord deepens, you will not feel at all that the Lord and the Holy Spirit are two. Instead, you will sense that the One who is working in you is the Spirit of life, the Lord Spirit. It is this Spirit who is doing the work of transformation in you by His life, nature, essence, and element. This is the experience in the Holy of Holies, in the spirit, in the deepest place.

I repeat, 2 Corinthians shows us the condition of a person who enjoys Christ while living in the spirit after he has truly entered into the Holy of Holies. This is a very deep experience, yet very few Christians today pay any attention to it. This one who is in the Holy of Holies does not care for any outward blessings; he does not care for the sunlight of the outer court. The environmental arrangement by God's hand has brought this person completely into the deepest part to live in the spirit. We may say that his outward being is completely stripped and utterly torn down. He has come to the point that he himself has no way at all. He is burdened excessively, beyond his power, so that he no longer has any confidence in himself or trusts in his wisdom. He is not at ease outwardly, and his prayers before the Lord for his circumstances are not answered. All these matters have turned him within to live in the spirit, that is, to live in the Holy of Holies, to enjoy God and experience Christ there. This is the main message of 2 Corinthians. Within such a person there are the constituting work, the writing work, the mingling work, and the transforming work of the Holy Spirit, which cause him to be transformed into the same image as the Lord from glory to glory.

I hope that you, brothers and sisters, would remember that 2 Corinthians chapter one says that we are excessively burdened, beyond our power, so that we trust not in our wisdom but in God's grace and in the God who raises the dead. Chapter two says that we are His captives. Chapter three says that He is in us doing the writing work, the constituting work, and the transforming work so that we may be transformed into the same image as the Lord. Chapter four talks about all kinds of attacks and ordeals to tear down the outer man so that the inner man, the regenerated spirit, may be renewed day by day. Chapter six also refers to various kinds of hardships; such a one is seemingly poor and seemingly cast down and has received not only good reports but also evil reports. Chapter eleven gives us a picture, showing that what such a person experiences seemingly is not blessing but afflictions. Chapter twelve has a special place in the Scriptures. The thorn will not be removed from you, but grace will be given for your experience. These are all the central threads in the book of 2 Corinthians. In order to know this book, you must know these chapters and verses. The central thought of this book is to bring a person completely from the outside to the inside. Such a one has been completely torn down outwardly, is altogether in the spirit, and has truly entered into Canaan, enjoying Christ as his grace.

A PARTICULAR CONCLUSION

Now we come to the conclusion of 2 Corinthians. The conclusion of this book is different from the conclusions of all the other Epistles. Most of the Epistles end with words such as "the grace of the Lord Jesus Christ be with you." But this book says it this way: "The grace of the Lord Jesus Christ and the love of God and the fellowship of the Holy Spirit be with you all" (13:14). This ending is very meaningful because this book is concerning the grace of God, which is simply Christ Himself.

You will remember that in chapter one Paul said that they were pressed by the sufferings that came upon them to such an extent that they could not trust in their wisdom but could only trust in the grace of God (v. 12). Moreover, in chapter twelve the Lord said, "My grace is sufficient for you" (v. 9). Then at the conclusion of chapter thirteen Paul said, "The grace of the Lord Jesus Christ...be with you all." When he said this word, he showed the source, the origin, of this grace. It is the love of God. According to the persons of the Trinity, Paul should have mentioned the love of God first, then the grace of Christ, and then the fellowship of the Holy Spirit. But here he mentioned the grace of Christ first, because this book is concerning grace. Grace is the subject of this book. However, when he mentioned grace, at the same time he showed us that the source of this grace is the love of God. Grace and love are not two separate things but two ends of one thing. On God's end, it is love; on Christ's end, it is manifested as grace. In other words, when the grace of Christ is traced back to its origin, which is God, it is love, and when the love of God is expressed through Christ, it is grace. Grace is the expression of love, and love is the source of grace. The grace of Christ comes out altogether from the love of God. Therefore, when Paul said, "The grace of the Lord Jesus Christ...be with you all," he then pointed out the source, which is the love of God.

Furthermore, it is through the fellowship of the Holy Spirit that this grace is able to reach us. The fellowship of the Holy Spirit is the transmission of the Holy Spirit. The grace of Christ comes out of the love of God, but how does this grace come into us? How is it conveyed to us? How is it transmitted into us? It is through the fellowship of the Holy Spirit. Therefore, the conclusion shows us that in order to enjoy the grace of the Lord we must be in the fellowship of the Holy Spirit, and as we are enjoying the grace of the Lord, we taste the love of God. Therefore, the Holy Spirit, the Lord Jesus, and God are not three separate Gods. In the same manner, these three—love, grace, and fellowship—are one. Today if you want to enjoy the grace of Christ, you have to be in the fellowship of the Holy Spirit, and as you are enjoying the grace of Christ, you will naturally taste the love of God. The three Persons are one God, and the three matters are one thing.

Let us use electricity as an illustration. With electricity, there are the source, the current, and the supply, which is the electricity itself. All of these are electricity. When you want to practically apply the electricity, you turn on the switch, and the electric supply comes and the electric current also flows, bringing with it the electric source. It is also the same with blood and blood circulation. The circulation of blood is simply the flowing of blood; it is not something other than the blood.

Therefore, the fellowship of the Holy Spirit is God Himself flowing. When the flow is hidden, it is love. When love flows out, it is grace. When grace flows into us, it is fellowship. This fellowship is by means of the Spirit, and this Spirit is altogether in our spirit. Therefore, today we must learn to turn to our spirit, to enter the Holy of Holies. Only when you enter into the Holy of Holies can you contact the Spirit of fellowship; only when you are in the Spirit of fellowship can you enjoy the grace of the Lord; and only when you are in the grace of the Lord can you taste the love of God. Hence, if you want to enjoy this, there is no other way except to return to the spirit, to come back into the Holy of Holies. Once you come back, you are in Canaan enjoying the riches of Christ. With respect to the Lord, the enjoyment of these riches is grace; with respect to God, it is love; and with respect to the Holy Spirit, it is a kind of fellowship in us.

CHAPTER SIX

THE SPIRIT IN THE FOUR BOOKS FROM GALATIANS TO COLOSSIANS

We may say that Galatians, Ephesians, Philippians, and Colossians occupy an important central position in the New Testament. Following them, 1 and 2 Timothy and Titus are near the conclusion of Paul's Epistles. The Epistles of Paul begin with Romans and 1 and 2 Corinthians; at their conclusion are 1 and 2 Timothy, Titus, and Philemon; and in the middle are these four short books. Here you see that the sequence arranged by the Holy Spirit is very meaningful.

GALATIANS

These four books—Galatians, Ephesians, Philippians, and Colossians—form a cluster and are inseparable. Galatians shows us how we must live by Christ, who is our life. First, it pleases God to reveal Christ in us (1:15-16). Second, it is God's pleasure to have His Son living in us (2:20). Third, it is also God's pleasure that we put on Christ (3:27). Christ is not only inside of us but also outside of us as a garment being put on us. Fourth, we need to let Christ be formed in us (4:19). For Christ to be formed in us means that Christ is able to spread in us and to constitute Himself into every part of our entire being. At first Christ only lives in us and is not able to extend or spread. Gradually, however, He now occupies every part within us by saturating and constituting every part of our being with Himself. Therefore, He is formed in us. Fifth, the book of Galatians shows us that Christ's living in us and being formed in us altogether depend on the Spirit. Therefore, we have to be in the Spirit, to walk according to the Spirit, and to live by the Spirit (ch. 5). We must be in the

Spirit; only then are we truly letting Christ live in us, only then do we truly put on Christ, and only then are we truly letting Christ be formed in us.

Finally, chapter six shows us that, before God, our being circumcised or not being circumcised does not matter. In other words, neither religious rituals, religious regulations, keeping the law, nor having good behavior are anything, but being a man of the new creation, being a new creation, is what matters. To be the new creation is to live in Christ by the spirit, to experience Christ by the spirit, and to live by Christ. This is different from the general religious concept in Christianity. The religious concept is that man should improve his behavior so that he can practice good deeds, and that he has to observe certain religious rituals, religious forms, and religious teachings. If a man is able to keep all of these, then he is considered to be up to standard. However, here it says that this is not the case. What God gives us today is not religion, not even Christianity, but Christ Himself. Christ is not a religion but a living person, a life, who has been revealed in us and who is living in us. And He wants us to live in Christ, to put on Christ, and to let Christ spread in us, constitute us, saturate us, and occupy us until He is formed in us. Then we should walk by Him in the Spirit. This is the book of Galatians.

However, it is a pity that when Christians read the book of Galatians, not many understand it to this extent. Many people have expounded Galatians, and of all the commentaries by Martin Luther, the one on Galatians is the most famous, which is also his masterpiece. Many consider his commentaries on Galatians as the best exposition. If you read it carefully, however, you will see that Luther did not say much about the Spirit, but instead greatly emphasized the matter of justification by faith. He should not be blamed for this because at that time what God committed to him was the matter of justification by faith. It is true that in Galatians there is justification by faith; there is no question about that. However, justification by faith is not the spirit, the life, the center of Galatians. Justification by faith is the "skin and hair" and the "skeletal structure" of Galatians. The soul of the book of Galatians is Christ in the Spirit being our life, which results in His becoming our living and in His changing our image so that we may become altogether a new creation in Christ. This is the soul, the crux, of the book of Galatians.

Dear brothers and sisters, Galatians 3 speaks of the blessing promised by God to Abraham, and that blessing is the Spirit! Read Galatians chapter three again, and you will see that the blessing that God promised to Abraham is God Himself and that the reason God can be the blessing to us who have received the promise is that He is Spirit. This God who is Spirit comes into us to be our enjoyment; hence, He is the blessing promised to us. The blessing promised by God to Abraham is that Abraham and his descendants would be able to enjoy God Himself through Christ and in Christ.

Galatians 3 is a very difficult chapter in the holy Scriptures. Very few are able to study this chapter thoroughly. Very few have seen that the blessing promised by God to Abraham is God in Christ being our portion through the Holy Spirit, and this Holy Spirit is not separate from God but rather is God Himself. God Himself is such a living Spirit in us as our blessed portion. Today when we gain, enjoy, experience, and live in the Spirit, we enjoy the very God Himself.

Therefore, we have to say again that the crux of the book of Galatians is the Spirit. It is right that we need to know justification by faith. It is right that we need to see that on the cross the Lord Jesus satisfied the righteous requirements of God and thus accomplished the work of redemption, and we also need to see that today when we trust in His work we are justified. However, we must not see only this much, but we must also see that we must enjoy Christ Himself. Today this Christ is in us, and He is the Spirit, so we must come into the Spirit. We definitely have to see that Christ is the Spirit, God Himself is Spirit, and the Holy Spirit, of course, is the Spirit. The Triune God is this very Spirit. Today this Spirit is the blessing promised by God to Abraham. Today if we have this Spirit, we have this blessing. If you live in this Spirit, you are enjoying this blessing. Therefore, we must come into this Spirit. This is the book of Galatians.

EPHESIANS

After Galatians is the book of Ephesians. Galatians is concerning Christ as our life, whereas Ephesians is concerning the expression of Christ, which is the church. Once again, in Galatians we see that Christ is our life, while in Ephesians we see that the church is the expression of Christ. When Christ lives in us, the church appears. What is the church? The church is the corporate expression of Christ. Ordinarily we pay too much attention to individually expressing Christ. Please remember, however, that in the Bible the emphasis is not on the expression of Christ individually but on the expression of Christ by the church as a corporate vessel.

Therefore, in the book of Ephesians various kinds of expressions are used to describe how the church is the expression of Christ. The first expression is that the church is the Body of Christ (1:23). A man's body is his expression. Today every one of us is expressed through our body. I know all of you by your bodies, and you also know me by my body. If today none of us had a body, and only our souls were here, there would be no way for us to express ourselves.

Then the book of Ephesians also says that the church is the fullness of Christ (1:23). *Fullness* also means expression. Following this it says that the church is the building of Christ (2:20-22). Christ Himself is the cornerstone, and this building is joined together with Him. Then it also says that the church is His bride (5:22-32).

The book of Ephesians uses at least these four expressions to portray what the church is to Christ. The church is the Body of Christ, the fullness of Christ, the building of Christ, and the bride of Christ. These four expressions show us that the church is the enlargement of Christ. The church comes out of Christ; she is not only joined to Christ but is the increase of Christ. Concerning these we all have a certain amount of understanding. It is sufficient that we only point these out in brief.

However, Ephesians also shows us that the reason that the church can be all these to Christ is altogether due to the fact that the church is in the Spirit. Therefore, the Spirit is particularly mentioned many times in Ephesians. The church can be Christ's Body, fullness, building, and bride because the church is altogether produced in the Spirit. Hence, today the church must be in the Spirit and live in the Spirit.

We may all remember that Ephesians says at the beginning that all the blessings God has given us are spiritual. Being spiritual means being in the Spirit. Then it shows us that the Spirit of God came into us as a seal and as a pledge. By His entering into us, the Spirit of God impressed God Himself as a seal in us. God Himself in us is the seal. In this way we were made God's inheritance. After speaking this word, the apostle immediately prayed, asking God to grant us the Spirit of revelation. We need this Spirit to know the church as the mystery of Christ.

Chapter two speaks even more strongly concerning the spirit. It says that the house is fundamentally being built in spirit. If it were being built in the flesh, it would be virtually impossible for the Jews and the Gentiles to be built together, because in the old creation the Jews are simply Jews and the Gentiles are simply Gentiles. But now they are all in one spirit and have therefore become one Body. Today, in order to know the church, we have to know the spirit and to live in spirit. Only in spirit can there be the Body, and only in spirit can there be the building.

Chapter three says that it is altogether by being in spirit that we are able to see the vision, the mystery, and the revelation. Verse 5 of chapter three says, "It has now been revealed to His holy apostles and prophets in spirit." The Chinese Union Version rendered *in spirit* as *through the Holy Spirit.* Actually, it is difficult to say whether the word *spirit* used in such a place denotes the Holy Spirit or our spirit. To be sure, this is the mingled spirit of two spirits, as we mentioned before. It is in this spirit that we are able to perceive and understand the mystery of Christ and the church.

Then in the last half of chapter three it says that God would grant us, according to the riches of His glory, to be strengthened with power through His Spirit into the inner man, that Christ may make His home in our hearts and that we may be filled unto all the fullness of God. This is also altogether a story of the spirit.

In chapter four the Body is mentioned. This is also due to the fact that the Spirit is in the church. Therefore, the oneness of the Body is the oneness of the Spirit. For this reason, we must be in the Spirit. This shows us that this Spirit will work in us subjectively to such an extent that He will occupy our mind to become the spirit of our mind. Remember that this is the accurate translation of 4:23. It is not as the Chinese Union Version says, that you be "renovated in your will"; rather, it should read that you be "renewed in the spirit of your mind." Now this spirit has become the spirit of the mind. When you are in the spirit of your mind, you are renewed.

Chapter four also mentions that this Spirit is the Spirit who comes into us as a seal and as a pledge. Our body has not been transformed yet, but we have already been sealed within with such a seal. Our body has not yet been redeemed, but we have already been given this pledge, this security, as a guarantee that one day our body will also be transformed, be redeemed. Thus, we will be transformed from the inside to the outside to be the same as the God of glory.

Chapter five says that we must be filled in spirit. We must be full of the Holy Spirit in our spirit. Then chapter six says that we need to pray in the spirit. This prayer means breathing. Today we need to breathe in the spirit so that we may be able to fight in the spirit.

By going over Ephesians in this way, you will realize that we have not paid much attention to the spirit in our regular preaching of the word. What we have been speaking mostly are the peripheral, superficial things; we have not touched the center. We merely talk about the frame; we do not talk about the life within. Very often we gave messages from the book of Ephesians, yet we did not touch the Spirit. This is wrong. The essence of Ephesians is also our spirit. According to Galatians, in order to let Christ be our life and to live by Christ, we must be in the spirit. According to Ephesians, in order for the church to be the manifestation, the expression, of Christ, she must live in the spirit. Galatians shows us how we have Christ as our life in the spirit and how we live by

Him in the spirit, while Ephesians shows us how the church must be in the spirit to be the manifestation, the expression, of Christ. All these are altogether in the spirit.

PHILIPPIANS

The book of Philippians shows us in a more specific way how we can experience this Christ. Philippians speaks altogether about the experiences in Christ and our experience of Christ. Therefore, the most important phrase is "the bountiful supply of the Spirit of Jesus Christ" mentioned in 1:19. It does not use the terms "the Spirit of God" or "the Holy Spirit"; rather, it says, "The Spirit of Jesus Christ." This is very meaningful. This is the Spirit of the One who was incarnated, became a man, lived on the earth, suffered ordeals and afflictions, died on the cross, was raised from the dead, and ascended to the heavens. The Spirit of such a One includes all these elements of His; hence, in this Spirit there is a bountiful supply. Therefore, in verses 20-21 Paul says, "Christ will be magnified in my body, whether through life or through death. For to me, to live is Christ." This is to practically experience Christ.

Then in chapter four Paul says, "I have learned" (v. 11), "I have learned the secret" (v. 12), and "I am able to do all things in Him [Christ] who empowers me" (v. 13). He had experienced and gained Christ.

The whole book of Philippians is concerning our pursuing of Christ. In verse 8 of chapter three Paul says, "I have suffered the loss of all things and count them as refuse that I may gain Christ." In verses 13b-14 Paul says, "Forgetting the things which are behind and stretching forward to the things which are before, I pursue toward the goal [which is Christ] for the prize [which is also Christ] to which God...has called me upward." How do you gain Christ and experience Christ? This is entirely a story of the Spirit.

Therefore, when we help the brothers and sisters, we need to help them to get into the Spirit. We must show them over and over that this all-inclusive Spirit, this Spirit with the bountiful supply, is actually Christ Himself, the Lord Himself. He passed through the processes of becoming flesh, becoming a man, living on earth, suffering earthly hardships and afflictions, dying on the cross, and being buried. Then He resurrected, ascended to the heavens, and entered into glory. After passing through all these processes, He has become the Spirit with all these elements to be our supply. He wants us to receive Him, to experience Him, and to enjoy Him. Satan's stratagem is to distract us with many things other than Christ. Therefore, we must learn over and over again to forsake all things that we may wholeheartedly pursue this Christ.

COLOSSIANS

The book of Colossians shows us that the enemy, by his craftiness, is doing the work of carrying us off as spoil. His intention is to carry us off from the Christ who is the Spirit, who is life, who is the Head. Satan uses all kinds of ways to capture us, to take us away from Christ. Sometimes he even carries people off as spoil through the messages we give, because he entices us to speak other things. You may have been utilized by Satan to carry people off as spoil by speaking other things to them, yet you were unaware of it and still thought that you were edifying them. The proper preaching of the word ought to bring people to Christ, yet your preaching, doing just the opposite, takes people away from Christ by turning their attention to things apart from Christ.

Brothers and sisters, I believe that you can remember that many things are mentioned in Colossians 2 which take people captive. Sin is not mentioned there because sin seizes only the weak Christians, the fallen Christians, and the sinning Christians. Sin cannot capture the Christians who pursue the Lord. The world is also not mentioned as a capturing factor. The things mentioned in chapter two which take people captive are things that have been disguised and have become very attractive, such as the worldly philosophy, the empty words of deceit, the elements of the world, and the traditions of men. These include certain kinds of preaching in Christianity. Some preaching in Christianity includes a certain amount of philosophy. What is philosophy? It is a kind of theory without Christ. Regardless of what kind of message you give, if

Christ is not in it, if it does not enable people to touch Christ and to enter into Christ in the spirit, then that is a philosophy. Of course, the philosophy mentioned in Colossians refers to Gnosticism, but the principle is the same.

Today if we take a look all around us, we shall see that in Christianity today many people are preaching philosophies which appear to be true but are not. They hang out the sign of Christ and the sign of the Bible, and they select a sentence from the Bible, but what they talk about are some doctrines without Christ. Under this principle, we have to be careful because it is very likely that we can also do this. We may receive some light from reading the Bible, find a topic from it, and begin to preach to others. Then when others listen to us, they may think that our speaking is quite good and has some inspiring power, yet in it there is neither Christ nor the Spirit. Please remember, this is also something included in Colossians 2. Unknowingly you may be used by Satan to take people captive so that they would not pay attention in their spirit to Christ.

Therefore, we all need to have an accurate perception. We need to learn to be in the spirit to have a great deal of experiences of this Lord who is the Spirit, and then when we go to release messages among the brothers and sisters, we will know from where we should speak and to where our speaking should lead people. We know the wiles of the enemy. He is not afraid of religion, not even Christianity. What he is afraid of is that man would enter into his spirit to touch this pneumatic Lord.

Today if you go and visit the United States, you will discover the extent to which Satan has taken people captive. We all know that today in Christendom the group which is most knowledgeable of the truth is the Brethren, yet you cannot believe how much the Brethren oppose the matter of the spirit, even to the uttermost. They simply cannot accept the truth concerning the spirit. Rather, they say that to speak about the spirit is to preach heresy. Most of the people in the Brethren assemblies do not acknowledge that our spirit is distinct from our soul. Instead, they say that the spirit is the soul, and the soul is the spirit.

Brothers, look at these four books. Christ in us is our life, and this results in His being our living; these matters are in the spirit. To be sure, we must help the brothers and sisters to see this. Christ lived out is the church, and the church is the expression of Christ; these matters also are altogether in the spirit. Furthermore, that we are able to personally experience Christ, enjoy Christ, and gain Christ is also completely in the spirit. Today we need to be cautious about one thing: Not only can sin and the world hinder us, but even religion, philosophy, doctrines in Christianity, and even messages spoken from the holy Scriptures all can be used by Satan to carry us off as spoil, preventing us from experiencing the pneumatic Christ in our spirit. These four books show us that we must be in the spirit to touch this pneumatic Christ and live by Him, thereby living out the one Body.

THE SPIRIT IN FIRST AND SECOND THESSALONIANS, FIRST AND SECOND TIMOTHY, AND TITUS

FIRST AND SECOND THESSALONIANS

Let us first take a brief look at the two books of Thessalonians. Because these two books are especially concerned about the Lord's coming again, they mention the matter of the Spirit only a few times. In these two books there is a statement that cannot be found in the New Testament nor in any other place in the entire holy Scriptures. This statement is in 1 Thessalonians 5:19: "Do not quench the Spirit." In these two books there is no particular light, particular discussion, or particular revelation concerning the Spirit, but there is a very solemn charge, which is to not quench the Spirit. After the other books have spoken about the Spirit, now here is a charge, a reminder: "Do not quench the Spirit." This word must be a reminder to us even today.

FIRST TIMOTHY

Now we come to 1 and 2 Timothy and Titus. We all know that when the apostle Paul wrote these books, the churches were already in desolation, had deviated from the right track, and had lost their original form. This was the background of these writings. In addition, Bible readers all acknowledge that these three books deal with the administration of the churches, and in the West some people called them the pastoral Epistles, the Epistles for the shepherding of the church. These observations are all correct. The background of these books is the deformation of the churches, and the content seems to be instructing people how to administrate the churches. However, I say again, the external things of the holy Scriptures appear to be one thing, but the core of the holy Scriptures is another thing. This may be compared to the way the body and appearance of a person are one thing, while his soul and life are another. The external matters, the superficial matters, of these three books were written under the situation of the churches' deformation, and they were for the administration of the churches. However, the contents, the center, the life, the soul, of these three books are still life and spirit. This is because the more the children of God are under the deformation and desolation of the churches, the more they need to know life and the more they need to live in the spirit. If we do not live in the spirit, and if we pay attention to outward, doctrinal discussions instead of paying attention to life, then the church will even more be in confusion. If we all absolutely focus on life and live deeply in the spirit, then the problems, disputes, and deformation will be gone. The reason that the churches are deformed is that they have departed from life and are not living in the spirit.

In these days we have been talking about washing each other's feet, blending with one another, loving one another, and coordinating with one another. Please consider this: If we neglect life and are not in the spirit but pay attention to doctrines and other matters, soon our coordination will collapse, and we will have problems with each other. Therefore, the central matters of the Epistles written by Paul under the decline of the church are altogether related to life. For this reason, in the two books of 1 and 2 Timothy, life is mentioned numerous times, and the spirit is also spoken of many times in a particular way.

Not Teaching Different Things

Let us first look at 1 Timothy 1:3: "Even as I exhorted you, when I was going into Macedonia, to remain in Ephesus in order that you might charge certain ones not to teach different things." If you read through 1 and 2 Timothy, you will see that *different things* refers to the things which were different from what the apostles preached and taught. What were the apostles preaching? The apostles preached that Christ, who is our Savior, comes into our spirit to be our life, thus issuing in the church as a great mystery. This is what the apostles preached and taught, but at that time there were certain ones who rose to teach other things. I absolutely believe that they were teaching the law and the Old Testament. They were not preaching a strange religion or the things of other religions. Instead, they were teaching the holy Scriptures, and their teachings were based on the Scriptures, yet what they emphasized was different from what the apostles emphasized. The apostles emphasized that Christ as our Savior and as our life produces the church as the great mystery of God, which is the house of God, the pillar and base of the truth. Another group of people were also teaching the Scriptures, but they had a different interpretation and were disputing with others. This kind of problem did not begin at the present time but had already begun in the first century.

Let us read on: "Nor to give heed to myths and unending genealogies" (v. 4a). *Myths* refers to the traditional things in Judaism. In the Jewish religion, besides the Old Testament Scriptures, there were many stories and beliefs handed down from the past, and people liked to listen to such things. Even today in the Catholic Church there are many such things, many legends. *Unending genealogies* refers to the genealogies in the Old Testament history diligently studied by the Jews. These seemingly were religious matters, and some of them were based on the holy Scriptures, but Paul said that these were different doctrines that produced questionings rather than God's economy, which is in faith. In the universe God has an economy, an arrangement, which is to be understood by faith. Hence, it is an economy, an arrangement, in faith. In other words, the message, the truth, which the apostle preached was God's economy throughout the ages. This economy of God is for Christ to be our Savior and our life that we may become His members coordinated to form a Body for the expression of God Himself. This is God's economy in our faith. In the early churches, however, some people other than the apostles were teaching the traditional things of Judaism and the genealogies of the Old Testament. However, these things only led to questionings; they did not reveal the mystery of God's economy. Therefore, Paul asked Timothy to charge those people not to teach those things anymore.

Allow me to say this: Based on this principle, sometimes we have to stop the speaking of some brothers in the church meetings, because their speaking will produce questionings in the church, which will not edify, establish, or supply the brothers and sisters and therefore will not be helpful to the economy of God. According to this principle, there is a basis for stopping people from carelessly speaking in the church. In other words, it is not that any brother can simply speak in the church whatever messages he chooses. Not to mention if he taught idolatry; even if he were to teach other things which are apparently taken from the Scriptures, his speaking still must be stopped. The speaking must unveil the mystery of the economy of God instead of stirring up problems among the brothers and sisters.

In the United States a brother once came to us and demanded, based on 1 Corinthians 14, that in the meetings if anyone has an inspiration, he must be allowed to speak, and that if we disallow him to speak, we are not keeping the teaching of 1 Corinthians 14. Initially, this argument seems to be reasonable. Then after referring him to 1 Timothy 1:3, I asked him, "When Paul charged certain ones not to speak, was he charging them not to speak in their homes?" Of course, the answer is no; it is obvious that Paul meant that those people were not to speak in the meetings. It is true that all Scriptures were written under the inspiration of God, but we must know that the New Testament revelations are not the same as the Old Testament revelations. Whereas the Old Testament revelations are purely divine revelations without involving human experiences, the New Testament revelations are based upon human experiences. Therefore, when Paul wrote the Epistles, he had had certain experiences, and his writings were based on his experiences. First Corinthians was written in the early stage of his ministry when he felt that in the meetings the brothers and sisters all can speak. Gradually, after a few decades when he wrote 1 Timothy in his old age, his speaking changed.

Let me give another example. In 1 Corinthians 7 Paul said that he wished that all the believers would remain unmarried even as he did, but when he wrote 1 Timothy 5, he said that he wished that the believers would be married. His speaking changed. In his early years of service he had the feeling that it was best for the believers not to marry but to be wholly for the Lord. After several decades, however, he observed that it was easy for the believers to get into trouble due to the weakness of the flesh, so he wrote another Epistle saying that it was proper for them to marry. Today we are not in the early stage or in the middle part of Paul's ministry. Rather, we are in a time which is many years after the completion of Paul's ministry. Therefore, we must not give undue emphasis to following the teaching in his early ministry. Instead, we should stress more his teaching in his final stage, because the teaching in the final stage was a mature teaching. This may be compared to a fruit. In 1 Corinthians the fruit was not quite ripe, but in 2 Timothy it had completely ripened. This does not mean that what he wrote in 1 Corinthians is not the word of God, just as we cannot say that because an apple has not ripened, it is not an apple.

In the same way, we are not saying that 1 Corinthians 14 should be put aside. Rather, we are saying that we should read it in conjunction with 1 Timothy 1:3. If the speakings of the brothers unveil the mystery of God, then praise and thank the Lord; of course, they all may speak. However, if someone stands up and speaks all kinds of irrelevant things, then we must advise him to stop. Today we have this situation among us. In the fellowship meetings, the brothers and sisters who have learned more spiritual lessons tend to give more consideration before they speak; they fear the Lord, and they carefully try to sense if it is of the Lord that they speak. While they hesitate, however, some of those who are very bold will take the opportunity to stand up and give a long talk. If you give such a one five minutes, he will speak ten minutes, and after that, he will still want to speak. What then should you do? This is a practical situation. Therefore, after having experiences in the churches over a few decades, Paul finally said that if some were to speak improperly in the church, they would have to be stopped.

Taking Care of the Conscience

Let us now go on to 1:18-19: "This charge I commit to you, my child Timothy, according to the prophecies previously made concerning you, that by them you might war the good warfare, holding faith and a good conscience, concerning which some, thrusting these away, have become shipwrecked regarding the faith." Brothers and sisters, please note that here it mentions the matter of conscience. This is related to life and spirit. In order to experience life and to live in the spirit, we must take care of the conscience, because it is the main part of the spirit. Therefore, when you take care of the conscience, you take care of the spirit for the most part. When you follow the conscience, you follow the spirit for the most part. Today the Lord is life to us in our spirit, so when we take care of our conscience, we take care of our spirit and live mostly in life. No one can know life and yet neglect the conscience, nor can anyone live in spirit and yet do things in violation of the conscience.

Therefore, although these two books mention the spirit only occasionally, they refer to the conscience frequently. This is because these two books are not concerned with doctrine but rather with experience. If we only talk about the spirit, that is doctrinal. But once we talk about the conscience, that is experiential. This is because whenever you experience the spirit inwardly, you will ask, "Is there peace within me? Do I feel at ease or not? Is there an inner harmony with God?" These are all stories in the conscience. If you take care of the conscience in this way, this proves that you are living in spirit. Therefore, *conscience* in these two books is simply another way of referring to the spirit. It is speaking of the spirit from experience in a more practical, specific, and real way.

If you like, in your interpretation you may use the words *conscience* and *spirit* interchangeably. Thrusting away their conscience, some have become shipwrecked regarding the faith. To thrust away the conscience is to abandon the spirit. When a brother speaks and acts carelessly, this proves that he has abandoned his spirit, no longer being in the spirit or caring for the spirit. However, when he particularly heeds the conscience, he is then living in the spirit. Therefore, Paul seemed to be saying to Timothy, "O Timothy, during this time of decline and confusion, you must learn and practice living in the conscience, that is, living in the spirit, and teach others to do the same thing. Don't just engage in outward discussions and arguments. Rather, learn to live in the spirit. Practically speaking, to live in the spirit is to take care of the conscience. Once you disregard the voice of the conscience, immediately you come out from the spirit. If so, you have become shipwrecked regarding the spiritual things of God."

Knowing the Church as the House of God

Then in 3:14-16 Paul said, "I write to you, hoping to come to you shortly. But if I delay, I write that you may know how one ought to conduct himself in the house of God, which is the church of the living God, the pillar and base of the truth. And...great is the mystery." This portion implies that the church is not an organization but the place where the living God dwells. Also, the church is not the support for a great number of doctrines or a great deal of biblical knowledge but upholds Christ as the pillar and base of the truth. Furthermore, the church is a great mystery, which is God being manifested in the flesh. Paul seemed to be saying, "O Timothy, if you know these matters and live in them, you will then truly know how to conduct yourself in the house of God."

Dear brothers and sisters, what does this mean? Please remember, this is life and spirit. Today it is not a matter of exhorting the elderly ones as fathers or as mothers, nor is it a matter of exhorting the younger ones as brothers or as sisters. Rather, you need to see clearly that the church is the place where the living God dwells and where Christ is being supported and that the church is a great mystery of God. Therefore, you must be a person who is in spirit and who lives in life. When you are exhorting others to be in the spirit and to live in life, the living God is there, Christ is being upheld there, and God is being manifested in the flesh. Therefore, this is a story of life and spirit.

It is a great pity that when the seminary students study these two books, they pay attention only to what the qualifications of an elder are and what the attitude of the Lord's servants in dealing with the elderly ones should be. These are all superficial matters. What then is the intrinsic matter of these books? It is the spirit of life. We need to learn to remain in the spirit that we may touch life. Only then can we be in the reality of the church and know how to conduct ourselves in the church.

Laying Hold on the Eternal Life

Following this, 6:12 tells us that we need to lay hold on the eternal life, which is the Lord Himself, God Himself. This is the life on which we must lay hold. In other words, we must live in this life. It is not living in interpretations or doctrines but living in the life which we have received. I have briefly pointed out these things to show you that 1 Timothy also speaks about the life in the spirit.

SECOND TIMOTHY

Fanning the Spirit into Flame

Therefore, in 2 Timothy 1:6-7 Paul said, "I remind you to fan into flame the gift of God, which is in you through the laying on of my hands. For God has not given us a spirit of cowardice, but of power and of love and of sobermindedness." What does it mean for you to fan your inner being into flame? This is nothing other than that you uplift the spirit. When your spirit is down and deflated, that means the flame in your inner being is going out. Now you need to fan your inner being into flame, to make it burning again. This is to lift up your spirit within. Here you see that what we need most is to exercise, to use, our spirit and not be influenced by our environment so that our spirit may be uplifted, burning, and inflamed.

The Indwelling Spirit Being a Guarding Spirit

Second Timothy 1:14 says, "Guard the good deposit through the Holy Spirit who dwells in us." Such an utterance cannot be found in the other Epistles. Our spirit, which is of power, of love, and of sobermindedness, must be fanned into flame. Furthermore, the Spirit of God is dwelling in us so that, through Him, we may guard the things God has committed to us. Such utterances in 1 and 2 Timothy are not doctrinal but altogether experiential. This tells us that during the decline of the church, not only should we have a strong spirit within, but we should also know that the Spirit who dwells in us is the preserving Spirit, the guarding Spirit. There should be an intimate fellowship between Him and us. When our spirit is strong, and we enjoy the Spirit's preserving and guarding, then we are living in spirit. In this way we can overcome the situation of the church's decline, the church's deformation.

The Lord Being with Our Spirit

Finally, the last verse of 2 Timothy says, "The Lord be with your spirit" (4:22). At the end of the book, Paul concluded with such a great verse. In the entire holy Scriptures, only this verse says so clearly that the Lord is with our spirit.

"The Lord be with your spirit." Who is the Lord? The Lord is the Spirit. Who is the Lord? The Lord is the life in the Spirit. The Lord is the Spirit and also the life. Today He is with you in your spirit. Therefore, it is useless for us Christians to listen to thousands of words and thousands of messages. We need only one thing; that is, we must remember that today the Lord is dwelling in our spirit and that He is our life, He is our Lord, and He is our all. In order to experience Him you must come into your spirit. This is the life in 1 and 2 Timothy.

TITUS

In Titus 3 the Spirit is referred to in a particular way. Verses 5 and 6 say, "Not out of works in righteousness which we did but according to His mercy He saved us, through the washing of regeneration and the renewing of the Holy Spirit, whom He poured out upon us richly through Jesus Christ our Savior."

These two verses speak of the Holy Spirit in a particular way. The indwelling Spirit not only affords us regeneration, but this regeneration afforded to us is a washing. This is not the washing away of our sins but the washing of our nature, our old creation. The precious blood can only cleanse us of our sins, our filthinesses; it cannot purge away the things in our nature, in our old creation. This kind of purging can only be accomplished through the washing of regeneration. Not only so, the Holy Spirit continues to do the work of renewing in us. Therefore, the washing of regeneration is a beginning, and the renewing of the Holy Spirit is a continuation. The more you live in the spirit, the newer you become day by day. Thus, the Spirit is continually doing the work of renewing in you.

Brothers and sisters, in the entire book of Titus these two verses are the most important verses. This is because this book shows us that the work of the Holy Spirit in us begins with the washing of regeneration, and from then on He continues to do the work of renewing, to renew our being, which is of the old creation, step by step. This is not a doctrine, nor is it a matter of correction. Rather, it is altogether the work of the Spirit within us.

THE NEED OF THE CHURCH TODAY BEING LIFE AND SPIRIT

Brothers and sisters, during the decline of the churches, what the different localities need are not messages on other matters, but messages on the line of life and Spirit. Therefore, I truly hope that while serving in various places, the co-workers will do more digging, gain more perception, and have more experiences concerning this point and this line. I also hope that by their speaking they will be able to release what they have gained and thus bring the brothers and sisters on toward the same direction. Therefore, we all need to pursue life and know the spirit and its two aspects. We must know the Lord as the Spirit, and we also must know the spirit of power, of love, and of sobermindedness in us. By this spirit and according to our conscience we live in the Lord, who is the Spirit. This will result in the church's being rescued in the time of decline.

If we depend only on studying the Bible to research truths and doctrines, then more confusion will be brought in to the church in decline. The more we research the biblical doctrines and the more we study the interpretations in letters, the more the church will suffer loss. We need to see today that when the church is in a deteriorated and deformed state, the way of salvation is not in letters or in doctrines but in life and spirit. We must bring people back from all the letters, from mere Bible researching, Bible reading, and Bible studying. We must turn their attention to the life within and help them to learn to live in the spirit.

In these few chapters we have covered Paul's Epistles from Romans to 1 and 2 Timothy and Titus. Of course besides these there are the Epistle to Philemon and the Epistle to the Hebrews. Since they are supplementary books, we will not cover them here. In summary, the Epistles of Paul are altogether the embodiment of the spirit. I hope that the brothers and sisters can find the marrow, the soul, of these Epistles. Now what we all need to dig out, to open up, and to know are not the skeletal structure and skin of these Epistles but the spirit and life within them. Although I have spoken much, these give the brothers only a line and an outline. I hope that from now on all of you would go and dig slowly; then you will see more and what you touch will be richer. When your experiences deepen, you will be able to have richer utterances.

About the Author

Witness Lee was born in 1905 in northern China and raised in a Christian family. At age 19 he was fully captured for Christ and immediately consecrated himself to preach the gospel for the rest of his life. Early in his service, he met Watchman Nee, a renowned preacher, teacher, and writer. Witness Lee labored together with Watchman Nee under his direction. In 1934 Watchman Nee entrusted Witness Lee with the responsibility for his publication operation, called the Shanghai Gospel Bookroom.

Prior to the Communist takeover in 1949, Witness Lee was sent by Watchman Nee and his other co-workers to Taiwan to insure that the things delivered to them by the Lord would not be lost. Watchman Nee instructed Witness Lee to continue the former's publishing operation abroad as the Taiwan Gospel Bookroom, which has been publicly recognized as the publisher of Watchman Nee's works outside China. Witness Lee's work in Taiwan manifested the Lord's abundant blessing. From a mere 350 believers, newly fled from the mainland, the churches in Taiwan grew to 20,000 in five years.

In 1962 Witness Lee felt led of the Lord to come to the United States, settling in California. During his 35 years of service in the U.S., he ministered in weekly meetings and weekend conferences, delivering several thousand spoken messages. Much of his speaking has since been published as over 400 titles. Many of these have been translated into over fourteen languages. He gave his last public conference in February 1997 at the age of 91.

He leaves behind a prolific presentation of the truth in the Bible. His major work, *Life-study of the Bible,* comprises over 25,000 pages of commentary on every book of the Bible from the perspective of the believers' enjoyment and experience of God's divine life in Christ through the Holy Spirit. Witness Lee was the chief editor of a new translation of the New Testament into Chinese called the Recovery Version and directed the translation of the same into English. The Recovery Version also appears in a number of other languages. He provided an extensive body of footnotes, outlines, and spiritual cross references. A radio broadcast of his messages can be heard on Christian radio stations in the United States. In 1965 Witness Lee founded Living Stream Ministry, a non-profit corporation, located in Anaheim, California, which officially presents his and Watchman Nee's ministry.

Witness Lee's ministry emphasizes the experience of Christ as life and the practical oneness of the believers as the Body of Christ. Stressing the importance of attending to both these matters, he led the churches under his care to grow in Christian life and function. He was unbending in his conviction that God's goal is not narrow sectarianism but the Body of Christ. In time, believers began to meet simply as the church in their localities in response to this conviction. In recent years a number of new churches have been raised up in Russia and in many eastern European countries.

OTHER BOOKS PUBLISHED BY
Living Stream Ministry

Titles by Witness Lee:

Abraham—Called by God	0-7363-0359-6
The Experience of Life	0-87083-417-7
The Knowledge of Life	0-87083-419-3
The Tree of Life	0-87083-300-6
The Economy of God	0-87083-415-0
The Divine Economy	0-87083-268-9
God's New Testament Economy	0-87083-199-2
The World Situation and God's Move	0-87083-092-9
Christ vs. Religion	0-87083-010-4
The All-inclusive Christ	0-87083-020-1
Gospel Outlines	0-87083-039-2
Character	0-87083-322-7
The Secret of Experiencing Christ	0-87083-227-1
The Life and Way for the Practice of the Church Life	0-87083-785-0
The Basic Revelation in the Holy Scriptures	0-87083-105-4
The Crucial Revelation of Life in the Scriptures	0-87083-372-3
The Spirit with Our Spirit	0-87083-798-2
Christ as the Reality	0-87083-047-3
The Central Line of the Divine Revelation	0-87083-960-8
The Full Knowledge of the Word of God	0-87083-289-1
Watchman Nee—A Seer of the Divine Revelation ...	0-87083-625-0

Titles by Watchman Nee:

How to Study the Bible	0-7363-0407-X
God's Overcomers	0-7363-0433-9
The New Covenant	0-7363-0088-0
The Spiritual Man 3 volumes	0-7363-0269-7
Authority and Submission	0-7363-0185-2
The Overcoming Life	1-57593-817-0
The Glorious Church	0-87083-745-1
The Prayer Ministry of the Church	0-87083-860-1
The Breaking of the Outer Man and the Release ...	1-57593-955-X
The Mystery of Christ	1-57593-954-1
The God of Abraham, Isaac, and Jacob	0-87083-932-2
The Song of Songs	0-87083-872-5
The Gospel of God 2 volumes	1-57593-953-3
The Normal Christian Church Life	0-87083-027-9
The Character of the Lord's Worker	1-57593-322-5
The Normal Christian Faith	0-87083-748-6
Watchman Nee's Testimony	0-87083-051-1

Available at
Christian bookstores, or contact Living Stream Ministry
2431 W. La Palma Ave. • Anaheim, CA 92801
1-800-549-5164 • www.livingstream.com